I.S.A.M. Monographs: Number 27

The Reception of Jazz in America

A NEW VIEW

JAMES LINCOLN COLLIER

I.S.A.M. Monographs: Number 27

The Reception of Jazz in America

in America

A NEW VIEW

JAMES LINCOLN COLLIER

Institute for Studies in American Music
Conservatory of Music
Brooklyn College
of the City University of New York

Published by the Institute for Studies in American Music
Conservatory of Music
Brooklyn College of the City University of New York
Brooklyn, New York 11210

CONTENTS

ACKNOWLEDGMENTS

I wish to thank Dan Morgenstern and his staff at the Institute for Jazz Studies, Rutgers University; Harold Samuel and his staff at the John Herrick Jackson Music Library, Yale University; Curt Jerde and his staff at the William Hogan Ransom Archive of Jazz, Tulane University; and the staff of the Library for the Performing Arts at Lincoln Center, New York City, for their ever-patient willingness to help me in many ways. I would like also to thank the following, who discussed with me various aspects of the present topic, offering many illuminating insights: John L. Fell, Curt Jerde, Gene Lees, James T. Maher, and Grover Sales. I am especially grateful to S. Frederick Starr, who read the manuscript and gave me many valuable comments. I owe a particular debt to Ron Welburn, whose pioneering study of early American jazz writing triggered my interest in the subject and gave me many important starting points. Finally, I must thank my editor, H. Wiley Hitchcock, whose relentless eye saved me from a number of errors, and who held me to canons of good scholarship. Needless to say, the opinions expressed in this work are solely my own responsibility.

I

The history of jazz has been plagued by two myths which have badly distorted both the nature of American culture and the process by which jazz evolved from a local New Orleans music into a national—indeed international—phenomenon. The first of these myths says that the American people, until relatively recently, have ignored or despised jazz, and that it lived its early years as a music of the black ghetto, appreciated elsewhere only by a handful of enlightened white critics and musicians. This myth has been rubbed so deeply into the grain of jazz history that it appears in virtually every book on jazz that touches on the early development of the music. It has been accepted and repeated not only by jazz writers with particular axes to grind but also by many otherwise reliable scholars. Neil Leonard, in his highly regarded *Jazz and the White Americans*, says, ". . . at first almost all the statements reported in the press condemned jazz."[1] Sidney Finkelstein, in one of the best books on jazz from the 1940s, says, "It was a social, communal, people's music, and it was a ghetto music."[2] Whitney Balliett says that jazz had been "ignored or misunderstood for its forty-year life" in the United States.[3] Frank Tirro, in a history from the 1970s, says that jazz "met with impassioned opposition from the Victorian pro-prohibition majority of white Americans."[4] Rudi Blesh, an influential critic from the 1940s, says, "Jazz is the music that the whites in New Orleans saw only as 'nigger music' . . . perhaps even to be danced to if the inferior black men of the orchestra sat on a platform with their faces to the wall."[5] Marshall Stearns, author of the first good history of jazz, says that the "solid middle class seemed to remain permanently unmoved" by jazz.[6] Leroy Ostransky, in a book from the 1970s, says, "Until the swing era, there was little mention of jazz in popular magazines of national circulation, and whatever notice jazz received in the daily press was—its scantiness notwithstanding—pejorative and a little absurd. . . . Critical onslaughts in books, journals, and magazines were, of course, the bulk of jazz criticism. . . ."[7] John Hammond says, "It was in the early Twenties that the music was first developed and at that time it was looked upon with horror, by managers, leaders, and cafe-owners alike."[8] He said elsewhere that black musicians "die of privation and neglect"[9] and repeatedly insisted that in 1933 he could not record jazz for Americans but had to record for the British market, the implication being that there was little market for jazz at home.[10] The important European critic Charles Delaunay summed it up when he said, "America seems most anxious to kill off this art which it has sired."[11]

These statements are completely representative of the general view of jazz, both of scholars and more casual fans. I have been unable to find, in comments about jazz published since 1940, a single statement that jazz was generally popular in the United States before some recent date.

The second myth which has clung like a burr to jazz history is the idea that it was first taken seriously by Europeans. Ina Dittke, in a recent issue of *Jazz Times*, says that American jazz musicians "could expect to be accorded much more reverence and respect in France than was forthcoming in their native land."[12] Whitney Balliett says that Hugues Panassié's early book *Hot Jazz* "put jazz on the map in Europe and in its own country."[13] The English writer Derek Jewell, in a biography of Duke Ellington, says that Ellington was "nurtured by Europe rather than his own country. . . ."[14] Delaunay says, "It is not altogether surprising that all its originality and promise were first discovered by the intellectuals of 'old' Europe, the French *avant-garde* to be specific. . . . Ten years before America interested itself in jazz there existed an entire literature and a wide European public which passionately followed the appearance of new [jazz records]."[15] Another English author, Peter Gammond, also writing about Ellington, says that it was rare when "a jazz work was better received in its country of origin than elsewhere."[16] John Hammond says, "England was a much better place for jazz than America" in the 1930s.[17] Eric Hobsbawm, writing under the name Francis Newton, says, "Paradoxical though it may seem, the specialized jazz public in the U.S.A. has always been relatively, and probably absolutely, smaller than in Europe"; and he adds that the American market for jazz records "in the black years from 1930 to 1934 was zero."[18] Robert Goffin, a Belgian who was one of the earliest European writers on jazz, says that "the European critics . . . showed the way to American jazz fans."[19] Ian Carr, in a recent biography of Miles Davis, says that in New York in 1949 Davis and Charlie Parker were "members of a small clique of musicians who had a tiny cult following. In Paris they were international celebrities whose every word and note carried weight."[20] John Hammond said in 1933 that Louis Armstrong, "although famous now in England. . .is virtually unknown to the theatre public [in the United States]."[21] Timme Rosenkrantz, a Danish critic, points out that "When Louis and his wife got off the train [in Copenhagen] the ecstatic fans carried them on their shoulders up the street [while] in his own country, at best, only his manager would meet him at the railway station."[22] Rudi Blesh says that "the first country to accord intellectual recognition to jazz" was France.[23] Even as late as 1987, Krystian Brodacki, writing in the Polish journal (and organ of the International Jazz Federation) *Jazz Forum*, said that in the 1950s and 1960s "many American beboppers were living in Paris, where their music received greater acceptance and recognition than in their own country."[24]

Once again, these statements are representative. I have not found one comment made after 1935 outside of my own writing and that of Gene Lees, claiming that jazz got better treatment at home than it did abroad. And yet jazz is seen everywhere as the country's most important contribution to the arts. How can this be, if the music has been despised so here? What are the facts?

To begin with, segregation of blacks from whites in the United States was never as total in the nineteenth and early twentieth centuries as many have assumed. The wall between the races was to an extent permeable. In the South, a considerable degree of social, economic, and even sexual intercourse between whites and blacks was taken for granted. White children frequently grew up playing with black children in their neighborhoods or on their farms. White males regularly had sexual intercourse with black women and sometimes took them as lovers; in fact, even during slavery a few white women took black lovers.[25] Southern whites were wholly accustomed from childhood to see blacks around the home as domestic servants, and were frequently in their charge.

In the North, contact between blacks and whites was considerably less than in the South, especially in rural areas, but there was plenty of it. Especially after blacks began to flood north around the turn of the twentieth century, tens of thousands of black women were employed as domestics and "nannies" in middle-class homes. Blacks and whites did not always share workplaces, but they did to some extent, especially as unskilled labor at the bottom of the job market.

Of particular importance to jazz history in this respect was the institution of the "black-and-tan" cabaret or dance hall, a regular feature of the tenderloin districts that existed in every major American city, and many smaller ones as well, in the earlier part of this century and before. New York's Tenderloin and (later) Harlem, San Francisco's Barbary Coast, New Orleans's Storyville, Chicago's Levee, and similar places in other cities all had black-and-tans where blacks and whites mixed on a basis approaching social equality—dancing together, conversing at a bar, sharing a bed.[26] Earl Hines, speaking of the Grand Terrace in Chicago, where he worked during most of the 1930s, said, "The audiences were mixed. Segregation never crossed anyone's mind."[27] The San Francisco musician Charlie Turner reported that in the 1920s "We played many places where the whites mingled with the coloured."[28] *Variety* reported that Small's in Harlem was "an all season playground. To see the 'high hats' [i.e. whites] mingle with the native steppers [blacks] is nothing unusual."[29]

I am not trying to claim that any but a tiny minority of white Americans really got to know blacks as individuals—as friends, lovers, spouses. My point is only that a large proportion of Americans were accustomed to dealing with blacks on a personal and often fairly close basis. Given this fact, it is not surprising that most Americans had litle trouble accepting blacks on stages and bandstands. The black entertainer had existed since well back into the eighteenth century, when slave owners frequently trained blacks to play musical instruments for dancing or took guests out to the cabins to see blacks dance.[30] However, the real boom in black entertainment came after the Civil War. The minstrel show, which purported to show life on the plantations, had become by that time a major part of American entertainment, and after Emancipation, when blacks were freer to travel and start their own businesses, a number of them went into minstrelsy, ironically working in blackface to preserve the old minstrel tradition.[31] When minstrelsy declined in the 1870s and 1880s, blacks continued on into the variety and vaudeville shows that were replacing it.

Then, beginning with Will Marion Cook's *Clorindy, or the Origin of the Cakewalk* (1898), blacks began producing musical shows for Broadway, for audiences, surprisingly, that were both black and white, although segregated in a divided theatre. Thomas Riis, in a study of early black theater, says:

> The period of theatre history from 1898 to 1911 was one of special significance for black actors, musicians and dancers. It saw a large number of all-black casts appearing in ambitious productions. It saw the rise of black-composed music as part of an accepted national song style and the commercial success of black song writers. It saw black companies on Broadway, and international tours featuring black stars.[32]

Riis adds that by 1906 over two hundred blacks were working in some fifty vaudeville acts. By 1913 whites were going to Harlem's Lafayette Theatre for "The Darktown Follies."

In particular, in the years after 1910 or so, blacks took a major role in supplying dance music for whites. The black musician Tom Whaley, later Duke Ellington's copyist, said, "Well you see, up till the First World War there was nothing but black musicians. White musicians didn't have a chance."[33] Whaley was speaking of Boston, but in New York the black bands of James Reese Europe, Ford Dabney, Luckey Roberts, and others were commanding many of the best "society" jobs. The Europe band became well-known after 1914 when it was the preferred backup for the famous dance team of Vernon and Irene Castle. And Roberts was even being brought down to Florida to play at Palm Beach for the very rich.[34]

By the time that jazz began to evolve out of its precursors in New Orleans after 1900, the black musician in a white night club, at a picnic of whites, or at even a private dance in a wealthy white home was completely accepted. Especially in New Orleans, where blacks were not generally physically segregated in ghettos but frequently lived next door to whites, the black was utterly familiar, and no surprise on a bandstand. In fact, as the New Orleans jazz authority Al Rose has pointed out, in New Orleans at that time it was *Italians* who had to go in by the back door of well-to-do white homes; blacks could use the front door.[35] As a consequence, New Orleans mainstream whites were hearing jazz as a matter of course even as it was evolving out of the blues, ragtime, and other types of music. They could hardly avoid hearing it as played in the streets in parades and on advertising wagons, or at the popular picnic grounds by Lake Pontchartrain. In any case, a substantial number of New Orleanian whites did not *want* to avoid jazz. White sports out on the town frequently visited black honky-tonks or the black parks, Lincoln Park and Johnson Park, in all of which there were jazz bands, among them the one led by the legendary Buddy Bolden. The black New Orleans bassist Pops Foster said, "You couldn't tell who [Lincoln Park] was for, there were so many whites there."[36] Hyppolite Charles, another black New Orleans musician, reported that he played many jobs at Tulane University, then entirely white.[37] Louis Armstrong with the Kid Ory band, also played many dances at Tulane.[38] King Oliver and Armand Piron played in white resorts at Spanish Fort, according to Stella Oliver.[39] Zutty Singleton, another New Orleans black, said, "We played for society kids on Saturday afternoons [and] we also played at the New Orleans Country Club and the Louisiana Restaurant, which was a fine, high-class place."[40] Black society bands, which played some jazz, like the Armand Piron and John Robichaux orchestras, regularly worked at important white locations like Tranchina's on Lake Ponchartrain. In fact, it has not often been made clear that the famous riverboats, which figure so largely in the legend of jazz, were restricted to whites, although occasionally on Mondays special trips would be held for blacks.[41]

In sum, many New Orleanians, right from the beginning, liked jazz and made a point of hearing it. Not all did, of course; one editorial in the *New Orleans Times-Picayune*, widely reprinted in the jazz literature, compared jazz to "the dime novel or the grease-dripping doughnut" and insisted that jazz pieces "are manifestations of a low streak in man's tastes. . . ."[42] What has never been pointed out in the jazz literature is that this editorial provoked a flurry of letters in support of jazz. One said, "It is the typical American music . . . filled with the spirit and bustle of American life"; another response was, "Whenever a person desires to pretend to more culture and refinement than his neighbors, he takes a fling at whatever the mass of folks enjoy, be it ragtime, jass, Douglas Fairbanks, comic supplements, popular novels, or even doughnuts."[43]

It is abundantly clear, then, that jazz, far from being despised, was well liked by a substantial proportion of the population of New Orleans before it became a national fad. Some people, of course, disliked it, but all the evidence suggests that the antis were a minority, and possibly a quite small minority at that.

Jazz musicians began to drift out of New Orleans as early as 1910 or thereabouts. Contrary to legend, they did not at first move up the Mississippi to Chicago but out to the West Coast, drawn by the climate; the new Southern Pacific Railroad, which was hiring blacks out of New Orleans to work as cooks and waiters in the dining cars; and a perception that there was somewhat less race prejudice there than in other places in the United States, which was probably true. During the succeeding decade a number of important New Orleans musicians based themselves on the West Coast for extended periods. Jelly Roll Morton, Bab Frank, Kid Ory, Wade Whaley, Mutt Carey, and some musicians associated with the legendary Original Creole Orchestra, which included Freddie Keppard, worked around Los Angeles and San Francisco, especially San Francisco's Barbary Coast district, which offered to jazz an ecological niche similar to the one it had left behind. In fact, the first published appearance of the word "jazz" seems to have been in a San Francisco newspaper in 1913: it reported that the San Francisco Seals, a minor-league baseball team, had brought to its training camp a band for its entertainment, and that the players had plenty of "jazz," which the reporter defined as "pep" or "enthusiasm."[44]

Interest in this peppy new music was fueled in part by a craze for dancing which began about 1910 and was a national fad by 1912. In these years a group of lively new dances were developed in low dance halls and black-and-tan cabarets—the Texas Tommy, the Grizzly Bear, the Bunny Hug, and a series of "trots" which eventually were subsumed under the name Fox Trot. These dances rapidly slipped into the mainstream of the culture and became immensely popular. The new jazz music seemed to be exactly right for them, so much so that the dances eventually came to be called "jazz dances."[45]

By 1915 or so the sports and night-lifers of the West Coast, as well as a good many tourists out for a night on the town, were familiar with jazz, which was being used to accompany the trots. But the real jazz boom took place in Chicago. In 1915 a club manager brought up to that city from New Orleans Brown's Band from Dixieland: the next year Stein's Dixie Jazz Band arrived.[46] These were both white groups, and worked in a number of the city's cabarets, among them the Casino Gardens, Schiller's Cafe, and Del Abbe. Brown's Band went on to play in the New York area for a time, probably early in 1916, and by the end of the year interest in the new music was spreading. In September 1916 *Billboard* referred to jazz as "vaudeville's newest craze."[47]

Enthusiasm for the music was such that in January 1917 the New York restaurant Reisenweber's, one of Broadway's most prestigious, brought in from Chicago the Stein band, without Stein and now called The Original Dixieland Jass Band. This was one of the major events in jazz history. The bandsmen had to acquire tuxedos to play in Reisenweber's, because, as the cornetist Nick LaRocca put it, "We were coming out of a dive, and going into one of the most fastidious and largest places in New York."[48] The Reisenweber engagement was a roaring success. Very quickly Victor recorded the group, and the recordings became best-sellers. Within a year the Original Dixieland Jass Band had got its price up to $875 a week,[49] an enormous sum for the time, and was billing itself as the highest-paid five-piece outfit in America, a claim that was almost certainly true. The music of the Original Dixieland Jass Band captivated thousands of young musicians, who immediately set about learning how to play jazz, among them such future jazz stars as Bix Beiderbecke and Benny Goodman, who imitated directly the cornet and clarinet players of the group. In addition, thousands of other musicians began incorporating into their music devices they copied from the Original Dixieland Jass Band and similar groups, in order to keep up with what appeared to be a fad. The Wilber Sweatman band, originally a vaudeville group featuring the leader playing three clarinets at once, was by 1918 playing such Original Dixieland Jass Band tunes as *Bluin' the Blues* in a close imitation of the New Orleans group.

How many jazz bands were working in the United States during the first years of the boom is difficult to know. Louis Metcalf, a New York trumpeter traveling with a show in 1921, said that there were jazz bands in almost every town they visited.[50] *Popular Mechanics* magazine in about 1922 said, "Now there are thousands of jazz orchestras in this country. Almost every town of 5,000 or more has one or more. Few vaudeville programs are complete without a jazz number."[51] As early as 1917 *Variety* said,

> Music is becoming more and more potent and prominent among the cabaret attractions. Gingery, swinging music is what the dancers want, and it often is looked for by those who do not dance. . . . The genuine "Jazz Band" at Reisenweber's, however, notwithstanding the sober opinion of it, appears to be drawing business there. Late

in the morning the Jazzers go to work and the dancers hit the floor, to remain there until they topple over, if the band keeps on playing.[52]

Another periodical, *The Dance*, said in 1917, "The jazz band idea is sweeping the country. Bands are playing jazz, cabarets are singing and dancing it, and dancing masters are teaching it. Wherever you go you hear jazz music."[53]

To be sure, many of these bands were ordinary dance bands that were incorporating into their music a few jazzy effects—trombone portamenti, imitations of animal sounds, a lot of noisy drumming—and by-play with mutes which was intended to be visually entertaining as much as anything. A comic or vaudeville element persisted in jazz for a decade, as the comedy in some of the classics by the Armstrong Hot Five suggests. But we should not be too quick to declare all these early jazz bands poor imitations of the real thing. The much-maligned Ted Lewis band of this early period was in fact a fairly good dixieland group, despite the leader's wobbling clarinet. Other now-forgotten groups like The Synco Jazz Band, which was recording in 1919, were also playing a reasonable version of dixieland. And the Original Dixieland Jass Band, playing the genuine article, continued to be one of the most popular and best-paid dance bands in America in the years after 1917. It is clear, from later recordings and memoirs of these early musicians, that a lot of them were getting the New Orleans idea: in New York a group around Phil Napoleon; in the midwest another group around Beiderbecke; in Chicago a group around Frank Teschemacher; and several others elsewhere were beginning to understand how jazz was to be played.[54] And these were only the best-known.

They were aided in learning by the fact that the jazz boom after 1917 drew up from New Orleans a lot of musicians, both black and white, who might otherwise have stayed home, as New Orleanians tended to do. Through the years 1917 to 1922 they flooded north, especially to Chicago and the West Coast: King Oliver, the Dodds brothers, Leon Ropollo, Paul Mares and others in the New Orleans Rhythm Kings, Wingy Mannone and Sterling Bose with the Arcadian Serenaders, Sidney Bechet, and eventually Louis Armstrong, forming informal schools at which the northern players could study. Nor was it just the northern whites who were finding out about the music from the New Orleanians: northern blacks like Bubber Miley were learning from King Oliver, Albert Wynn from the white George Brunis, Buster Bailey from the white Larry Shields, and eventually everybody from Armstrong.[55] By 1923, when jazz began to be recorded in substantial amounts, there were hundreds of musicians in America who could play it.

By this time jazz had escaped the low dives where it had mainly been played in the earliest years. Apologists for jazz have often pointed out that the music was not played in brothels, and associations with sex were mistaken. This was more or less true of the New Orleans period; but as the music began to move north and west, it was being played in the main in cabarets and dance halls populated with prostitutes, despite occasional forays into vaudeville, and the impression that the music was somehow related to sexual sin was generally accurate. Now, however, with the success of the Original Dixieland Jass Band at a prestigious restaurant, the music was seen as more respectable. By 1918 the group was playing for Catholic War Fund benefits put on by the parish of St. Francis de Sales in New York; for Liberty Loan drives; for fraternity and sorority weekend parties at good colleges. In October 1918 it played a fancy dinner dance at the Hotel Astor for the crew of the U.S.S. *Charleston*, with a menu including Crab Flakes à la ravigote, Boneless Squab, and Chicken Virginienne.[56]

Not everybody liked the music, of course. Two groups in particular opposed it: some music teachers and some members of the music "establishment" in general, who were afraid that jazz would drive out "good" music; and the conservative moralists who quite correctly saw that jazz was part and parcel of an anarchistic new feeling in the American air which was bringing with it salacious dances, sexual freedoms, and public drinking by the middle class. A few communities banned—or attempted to ban—jazz dancing, and some groups railed against the music, among them the Methodist Episcopal Church and the Federation of Women's Clubs. But the antis were distinctly a minority, as they themselves recognized. In 1920 a writer in the *Living Age* called jazz "a sound more indicative of Hell than of Heaven" but added, "Such music is the order of this barbarian day, and the minority can do little but endure."[57] In fact, it was more the dances associated with jazz than the music itself that concerned the moralists.

Contrary to what has been said by virtually every jazz writer who has touched on the subject, the American press generally supported jazz, if only because it has never been in the business of attacking fashions that appeal to its readers. The *New York Times*, for example, routinely reported the sermons and statements of the antis, and the town council votes to ban jazz; but its own stance toward the music was mildly approving. As early as 1919 the *Sunday Times Magazine* included a long article excoriating the world of serious dance for ignoring jazz,[58] and over the next ten years it ran 189 articles on jazz, in addition to more than 100 others in the early part of the 1910s on the controversy over the "jazz dances." The paper itself never editorialized against jazz, and the special articles it ran in the Sunday *Magazine* and elsewhere were invariably favorable.

Other newspapers were just as interested in the new music. In 1918, for example, the *New York American* gave its readers instructions on how to dance "The Jazz";[59] another paper reported in 1918 that jazz records were being placed on American troop ships bound for France;[60] and there were dozens of similar items. As early as 1917 the *New York Sun* ran a two-page spread on the Original Dixieland Jass Band. The writer found the music too noisy for himself, but admitted that it was popular:

> On the dancing floor of the resturant the couples gyrate with every sign of satisfaction, though there is no evidence that they have cotton in their ears. They smile happily as they dip and sway, holding each other after the most approved jiu-jitsu principles. . . . This latest musical craze that has struck a section of New York—and struck it giddy. . . . Authorities are particularly one in the view that this concord of swift sounds began its infant caterwaulings in this country at the Louisiana City [New Orleans]. Inundating the South like a bad break in a Mississippi levee, it was soon rampant in the underworld resorts and gradually worked its way up the river to Chicago, where most persons like their music raw.[61]

The article credited "negroes in the South" with the invention of jazz.

Magazines, too, ran the sermons of the antis, and a few of them editorialized against jazz, but the majority of magazine pieces about the music were approving or at least neutral. In 1917 the *Literary Digest*, a major weekly of news and opinion, ran an analysis of jazz rhythms (see p. 31 below) and continued to print pieces on jazz occasionally thereafter; for example, in 1919 it printed a respectful interview with the black bandleader James Reese Europe on the origin of the term "jazz" (Europe had it all wrong).[62] Between 1917 and 1929 leading American magazines would run over 100 articles on jazz, only a small minority of them hostile to the music.

This press coverage of jazz was not a continuous roar. The *New York Times* was reporting on the music only two or three times a month, on the average, and the magazines that were interested in jazz at all did not feature it more than once every two years or so. The fact is, however, that the American press was not hostile toward jazz but treated it as it usually does any broad national phenomenon—reporting on its controversies and trends, and offering its readers as much discussion of it as it thought they wanted.

How big the following for jazz was in the United States by, say, 1921, is difficult to estimate, especially since a lot of the music that Americans took to be jazz was only dance music pepped up by a few jazz effects. Although probably a majority of Americans went out dancing to jazz or jazz-oriented dance music at least occasionally, and a considerable minority went dancing several times a week—in a day before mechanical entertainment, dancing was a major social activity—probably only a minority of Americans really appreciated jazz, and had some idea of what it was. But it was not a small minority, as the success of the Original Dixieland Jass Band and its imitators substantiates. By 1919 *Music Trade Review* was saying, "To-day jazz music and jazz dancing are not novelties. They are accepted by the public at large. Their apostles run into the thousands, and their disciples into the millions."[63] It is certainly reasonable to estimate that by the first years of the 1920s, which would come to be called the "Jazz Decade," millions of Americans liked jazz, and knew in a fair way what it was.

II

It is critical to our understanding of early jazz and American culture to recognize that by far the largest proportion of the American audience for the music consisted of mainstream whites drawn from the whole spectrum of society, from the upper crust looking for new thrills down to working people paying a nickel a dance in the jitney dance halls. Although white entertainers performed for black audiences more frequently than has been realized, it was nonetheless rare for a white band to play at a black dance or party. Almost the entire audience for the early white dixieland bands was white. America was a racially segregated country. The places where such bands as the Original Dixieland Jass Band, the New Orleans Rhythm Kings, the Arcadian Serenaders, Bix and the Wolverines, the Original Memphis Five, and other white groups were usually playing did not in this period admit blacks, except perhaps, rarely, a well-known entertainer.

Blacks, on the other hand, were playing for both black and white audiences. Lincoln Gardens in Chicago, where King Oliver was playing (with Louis Armstrong on second cornet) in 1922 and 1923, was a black dance hall, and there were similar places in most big northern cities. But most of the early black jazz bands were playing either for white audiences or in black-and-tans for mixed audiences. Purcell's on the Barbary Coast was a black-and-tan; The Dreamland Cafe, and the Sunset Cafe, where Armstrong led his first bands, were black-and-tans;[1] clubs like Small's and the Nest in Harlem were black-and-tans.[2] And even the supposedly all-black places attracted some whites. Lincoln Gardens in Chicago was particularly a magnet for young white jazz fans. Jimmy McPartland remembers being taken there, with Benny Goodman, by Northwestern University students;[3] Lil Armstrong recalls seeing the white boys staring up at the band.[4] Bud Freeman reported spending hours at Lincoln Gardens and added, "Musically sensitive whites who had an opportunity to hear jazz were usually deeply affected by it."[5] When the management realized that there was white interest in the Oliver band, it began putting on regular "midnight rambles" for audiences of whites, principally the Chicago musicians who were struggling to learn the new jazz music.[6] (The midnight ramble for whites in black vaudeville theaters was a common institution, especially in the South, during the period. Bessie Smith performed in at least one.)[7]

These black jazz bands were performing for all-white audiences, as well as at black-and-tans. As we have seen, black bands had played for whites well back in the nineteenth century, and they continued to do so. The Original Creole Orchestra, with Freddie Keppard, toured vaudeville circuits in 1915 and probably earlier; the Oliver band was working a white jitney dance hall on the West Coast in 1921, and went on to play the Pekin Theatre, an after-hours club for gangsters and entertainers, mainly white, on its return to Chicago.

It is also true that a substantial, if incalculable, number of early jazz records were being bought by whites. A great deal has been made in jazz literature of so-called "race records" aimed at the black market, and the impression has been left that these early jazz records were bought only by blacks. A number of things needs to be said on this point. For one thing, the word "race" in reference to blacks was not pejorative; it was a term blacks insisted upon and used in their own newspapers. For another, although some special race catalogues were issued from time to time, this was solely for the convenience of black record-store owners and their buyers; all the early jazz records were also routinely listed in the regular record catalogues.[8] Finally, the issuance of special record series for the black audience was a temporary phenomenon which began around 1924 and dwindled away towards the last years of the decade. The first jazz records, those made by the Original Dixieland Jass Band and its followers, were meant for a white audience and were bought by it, and so were the bulk of the jazz records by the bands that followed, like the Wolverines, the New Orleans Rhythm Kings, and the Memphis Five. Indeed, whites were buying a lot of the records ostensibly aimed at blacks. Sherwood Mangiapane, a New Orleanian bass player, has reported that in the 1920s he had no difficulty buying Armstrong's early records.[9] In the 1920s Dave and Jack Kapp, later to operate Decca Records, had a record store on the edge of black Chicago.

> Negroes were the first to buy [race] records but soon white boys and girls came, and listened by the hour. The store was like an outpost on a mysterious, perhaps dangerous, frontier. Among those who came often, staying long, was Carl Sandburg. White musicians, music students, came to listen.[10]

We must realize that a considerable minority of blacks were opposed to jazz—probably a larger percentage of them than among whites. Religious blacks, especially members of the gospel churches which figured so largely in black culture, saw jazz and the blues quite specifically as "the devil's music." Young people from such families were frequently driven out of their homes for associating with such music. This happened, for example, to Lawrence Brown, one of Duke Ellington's premier soloists, when his preacher father gave him the choice of giving up dance music or leaving the family; Brown, who in later life never smoked, drank, or gambled, left.[11] Lil Hardin, pianist with King Oliver and later Louis Armstrong's second wife, reported that her mother called the blues "wuthless immoral music, played by wuthless, immoral loafers expressin' their vulgar minds with vulgar music";[12] as a youngster Lil had to sneak out to play. As early as 1925 Carl Van Vechten noted that blues "are looked down upon, as spirituals once were, especially by the Negroes."[13]

In addition, a huge percentage of American blacks of the period still lived in southern cabins without electricity or running water and were far too poor to buy many records, much less machines to play them on. Furthermore, these rural blacks did not have much contact with jazz, which was an urban phenomenon. Their music was the blues or gospel music and their knowledge of jazz was limited. Even in the north, urban blacks could not afford to spend much time at the popular black-and-tans where the famous jazz musicians were working. At the time, blacks constituted only about ten percent of the American population. Huge percentages of them—perhaps as many as half—were disbarred from supporting jazz for religious, economic, and cultural reasons. Jazz could not have survived as anything but a tiny local music had it been forced to depend mainly on finding a black audience. From the beginning it was the white audience that provided the economic base for it.

One major element in establishing jazz as part of the American cultural mainstream was a new spirit that was ranging through American life. This is far too complex a subject to deal with in any depth here. Suffice it to say that beginning about 1890 there was, as Lewis A. Ehrenberg says in his study of New York cabaret life, "a profound reorientation in American culture, one that broke from older forms of gentility in which individuals were to subordinate themselves voluntarily to a social code."[14] To put it simply, in this period Americans, especially young ones, were determined to throw off the constrictions of the older sexual, social, and artistic codes. A new wind was thought to be blowing; human life would be freer, more expressive. Edmund Wilson said expressly, "In repudiating the materialism and priggishness of the period in which we were born [the 1890s] we thought we should have a free hand to refashion American life as well as to have more fun than our fathers."[15] It is no accident that jazz, the Broadway musical, the movies, Tin Pan Alley, and the new dances all came into being at about the same time.

Jazz was seen quite specifically as reflecting this new spirit. It would be one of the weapons in the battle against the old worn-out morality. Frank Patterson, writing in 1922 in the *Musical Courier*, a classical music magazine, said,

> [Jazz] expresses our American nature—and as long as our nature is expressed by anything so simple and straightforward we will have no cause to worry. When our nature becomes so complex that we need the high art of Europe, or something similar, to express it, it will then be time to realize that we are getting old and effete.[16]

Another writer said in *The Nation* in 1922, "It is vulgar but it is healthily frank—as frank as the conversation of a group of young people who cleanly and intelligently discuss birth control."[17] To this new generation, going out to drink and dance to a jazz band carried with it the air of a crusade, of a moral battle of the bright new future against a dead past.

Another force propelling jazz into the mainstream was a boom in black show business.[18] This is also too large a subject to be accommodated here. However, increasingly through the years after World War I, blacks were seen as more expressive and in closer touch with their feelings than the more inhibited whites, and as having something to offer them. In particular, blacks seemed to many people to have a natural gift for song, dance, and comedy. Black entertainment grew more and more popular, and black jazz bands became correspondingly popular as well.

Thus a number of forces in American society, aside from attractions of the music itself, were pushing jazz forward. However, by 1922 or so what was meant by the term "jazz" was coming into dispute. When the jazz wave first broke over the country, all jazz bands were formed on the New Orleans, or dixieland, model: five- to seven-piece ensembles playing a contrapuntal, advanced ragtime with blues inflections and an increasingly looser rhythmic feel. All references to "jazz" meant this dixieland music, or at least the attempts to play it by the musicians apprenticed to it. But by 1921 a new form of jazz was being developed, principally by whites.

The key figure, whose role in the making of jazz has been entirely forgotten, was Ferde Grofé. He was born in New York City in 1892, exactly at the right moment to become a carrier of the new spirit that was to shake America. Grofé's father was a singer and actor. His maternal grandfather, Bernhardt Bierlich, was solo cellist with the Metropolitan Opera in the 1880s; his uncle, Julius Bierlich, was concertmaster of the Los Angeles Symphony; and his mother was also an accomplished cellist.[19] Grofé began the study of the piano at five, composition at nine. (There is a report that he studied in Leipzig as a boy, where his mother had also studied.) At fourteen he ran away from home for reasons that are obscure, worked as an itinerant laborer in Western mining camps, and played piano in dance halls as well. On his return to the family in San Francisco in 1909, he joined the Los Angeles Symphony. This was not a full-time job, and to support himself he worked in dives of the Barbary Coast.[20] Thus, by the time he was in his early twenties he was thoroughly at home in both classical music and the new hot music drifting out from New Orleans.

Sometime after 1914 Grofé made an association with a drummer named Art Hickman, who was leading a dance band in the fashionable St. Francis Hotel. It was certainly Grofé, and not Hickman, who invented a formula for the band which became a basis for the big jazz band that would dominate American popular music for three decades thereafter. It may have been Hickman who decided to build his band around a "choir" of saxophones, novelty instruments then having a considerable vogue, but it was undoubtedly Grofé who worked out the system of playing off other instruments in the orchestra against the saxophones in a vaguely contrapuntal fashion. (The Hickman group eventually consisted of two saxophones, trumpet, trombone, and violin, and a rhythm section of piano, drums and banjo.) This was not so much the angular counterpoint of the dixieland bands, in which two or three lines were sharply divergent, but tended to be somewhat more parallel accompanying lines. Grofé was also the one who came up with the idea of the dance-band "arrangement." Until this time bands had generally played chorus after chorus of the tune in the same way, for as long as was required. It was Grofé's idea to vary the music from chorus to chorus, now poising the saxophones against a trombone line, now allowing the banjo to solo, now pitting the trumpet against the saxes.

Sometime about 1919, Grofé fell in with a man who had a background similar to his.[21] Paul Whiteman was the son of the conductor of the Denver Symphony Orchestra, and a trained musician. In 1914 he was playing with the San Francisco Symphony. Whiteman was something of a scapegrace who spent a good deal of his time in the Barbary Coast drinking and womanizing, and he may have known Grofé from this period.[22] In any case, like Grofé he knew both classical music and jazz. In 1919 he formed an orchestra on the Hickman model, with Grofé as pianist and arranger. Although the Hickman orchestra made a major impact on the music business after a 1919 trip to New York, it was Whiteman's orchestra which became the model for the modern dance band. Grofé's arrangements for Whiteman of *Whispering, Japanese Sandman, Avalon,* and scores of other songs, became enormous sellers in 1920 and the years just after, and they made Whiteman the most celebrated bandleader of the period. Grofé's role was rapidly forgotten. By 1931 one writer referred to him as "the ghost writer" of jazz.[23] But Henry Osborne Osgood, who wrote an early book about what came to be called "symphonic jazz," said that the Hickman group was "the first complete modern jazz combination" and that Grofé was "the father of modern jazz orchestration."[24] Another writer said that he "undoubtedly was the first to reduce jazz to note and score."[25]

Whiteman, who had a genius for self-promotion, began announcing that he was presenting not mere dance music but *symphonic jazz,* a new art form of which he was king. To prove his point, in February 1924 he put on a now-legendary concert at Aeolian Hall in New York, at which he presented a piece of symphonic jazz commissioned for the occasion, George Gershwin's *Rhapsody in Blue*, which Grofé had orchestrated. (Whiteman had got the idea for the concert from a recital the previous year given by the well-known singer Eva Gautier, in which she included some Gershwin, Berlin, and Kern songs as well as her usual classical repertory. The Gautier concert gained a good deal of press attention.)[26] *Rhapsody in Blue* had little to do with real jazz, as many critics recognized at the time, but to the public it was final proof that this smoother, more refined jazz was America's contribution to the arts, part of the new, enlightened spirit awake in the land.

Almost immediately other leaders began to follow in Whiteman's enormous wake, among them Vincent Lopez, Irving Aaronson, Paul Ash, Paul Specht, and Leo Reisman, all of whom became celebrated bandleaders in the early and mid-twenties.

From about 1921 or 1922 American press interest in jazz became focused on the symphonic version; its biggest exponents were seen as Whiteman, Gershwin, and Irving Berlin. For several years after 1922 virtually everything that appeared in the general press about jazz referred to the new, symphonic version. For example, in a full-page piece in the *New York Times Book Review and Magazine* in 1922, Helen Bullitt Lowry extolled symphonic jazz and Whiteman, and said,

> Echoes of phosporescent jungle nights are there, too. But the raw jungle emotions are clothed now in the glamour that distance lends. Jungle music is undergoing a refining process under the fingers of sophisticated art. . . . It might be called good music in slang—as O. Henry was good literature in slang.[27]

Henry Osborne Osgood claimed that the new music was driving out the "ear-wracking hot jazz [that had] dominated the field for several years."[28] These comments are typical of dozens of others about the turn jazz had taken. Whiteman grew rich and published an autobiography which was serialized in one of the country's most popular magazines, the *Saturday Evening Post*. Others got rich along with him. By 1922 Vincent Lopez was commanding $5,000 a week for his orchestra, a huge sum for the time, and Whiteman himself was paying his star clarinetist, Ross Gorman (who was to work out the opening clarinet cry to *Rhapsody in Blue*) an astounding $400 a week.[29] It will stun musicians today to be told that, in a day without mechanical entertainment, so great was the dance-band boom that leaders scrambled to compete for the best musicians, or indeed musicians who could play at all. Abel Green, writing in 1922 for a New York show-business paper, *The Clipper*, said that, "according to the men who are booking orchestras all over the country there is an acute shortage of Class A dance orchestras at the present time."[30] The same year he reported that musicians in the better-known orchestras were earning from $75 to $300 a week.[31] By 1925 *Billboard* was reporting that there were six hundred jazz orchestras in New York alone, that top bands were being paid $10,000 a week, and that "Any fellow in this line today who has ability will not be able to accept all of the work offered to him."[32] Parenthetically, this demand for musicians made it possible for men who could not read music to work in bands and even to form them, and this in turn allowed many of the early jazz musicians to practice their art in public.

There is no question that Whiteman's version of jazz was preferred by a large proportion of the American public. But there was an awareness that there was a hot version, which a substantial number of Americans liked. Abel Green, in his regular column on dance music in *The Clipper*, wrote in 1924, "King Oliver, Negro jazz trumpeter, is the 'hottest' jazz musician of his kind in the business. He has set the pace which all the jazz cornetists with the crack bands follow."[33] At various times Green had praise for Bubber Miley and others. A more important show-business paper, *Billboard*, had by 1923 hired a black writer named James A. Jackson to cover the growing black branch of the entertainment industry. Jackson was no specialist in jazz—he was less knowledgable than Green (who was white)—but he gave black jazz musicians the same sort of serious coverage he gave to actors and dancers and at one time or another mentioned Alberta Hunter, Earl Hines, the Washingtonians (who would become the Ellington orchestra), Fats Waller, Jimmy Harrison, Trixie Smith (who was doing so well she was speculating in property in Flushing), Mamie Smith, Henderson, Johnny Dunn (with a photograph), Valaida Snow, Bessie Smith, Clarence Williams, Charlie Johnson, Luckey Roberts, Sidney DeParis, and others.[34] In early 1925 Jackson reported that the Oliver band had lost its library in a fire,[35] and shortly afterwards that "Buster Bailey and Louis Armstrong have been added to the Fletcher Henderson band, which is the talk of the dancing folk on Broadway.[36]

Jazz was also being covered by a magazine called *Orchestra World*, which seems to be unknown to all but two or three jazz scholars. It began in June 1925. It was a trade paper for the dance-band industry, was fundamentally in the symphonic-jazz camp—not surprising at a time when Whiteman, et al. dominated popular music—and the bulk of its pages were devoted to the Whiteman type of band. However, it was well aware of the hotter forms, and routinely included the Ellington, Henderson, Elmer Snowden, and Charlie Johnson groups in its list of "America's Leading Orchestras." (The list was heavily biased toward New York-based bands, but the Chicago-based King Oliver band made the list at times.) Its gossip column at one time or another mentioned such people, now seen as jazz pioneers, as Oliver, Miff Mole, Eddie Lang, Bennie Moten, Jelly Roll Morton, and Earl Hines. It did not do much record reviewing, but at times it praised recordings by Bessie Smith, Clara Smith, Henderson, Ellington, and others. In 1925 *Orchestra World* ran a full-page, quite respectful profile of Henderson, with a picture.[37] It said flatly, "There is no better dance orchestra than Fletcher's, white or colored." It gave W. C. Handy's book *Blues* a long, laudatory review; it carried a brief paragraph on Benny Carter's marriage; and it wrote of Duke Ellington, before he became nationally famous at the Cotton Club,

> So much of the charm of Duke Ellington lies in the grace of his musical translation that it is difficult to describe in cold, prosaic words. The lucently rippling style of his Washingtonians always scores heavily because it has a thrilling thread woven through it.

Of particular interest was a series of popularity polls that *Orchestra World* ran for a while in 1931, presumably to boost circulation hurt by the Depression. Most of those at the top of the lists were ordinary dance bands; but Ellington's group ran second or first most of the time, and important jazz musicians like Sonny Greer, Bubber Miley, Red Nichols, Steve Brown, and King Oliver also made the list, some of them high up on it.[38] It must be realized that by this time jazz bandleaders like Oliver and Nichols had national reputations in America, at least among those who followed popular music more or less closely.

Thus, although Whiteman's symphonic jazz was the dominant form through the mid-1920s, the hotter forms continued to hold a substantial audience. Through the mid-1920s, bands still working mainly in the dixieland mold, like those of King Oliver, Jelly Roll Morton, Red Nichols, various groups including Beiderbecke and his sidekick Frankie Trumbauer, and many others, actually increased in popularity. Although by 1927 Beiderbecke was working in big bands, his records of that year were dixie-based. So were those of Morton, Goodman's recordings of 1928, and many others. In fact, the publicity attending symphonic jazz, indiscriminate as it often was, helped to carry the older music along with it. As Neil Leonard has pointed out, touters of symphonic jazz gave the music as a whole a respectability it had not had before. "In large measure it was through their efforts that the term 'jazz' became in the twenties and thirties associated less with the brothel and more with the concert hall as a native product of which Americans could be proud."[39]

But the success of the Whiteman band and its followers was really too much for the older music to overcome. By the mid-1920s it was clear to most bandleaders that the public preferred its jazz arranged for big bands. New bands, like those of Fletcher Henderson and Duke Ellington, played from arrangements almost from the start, whether written-out or "head" arrangements worked out in rehearsal and memorized. King Oliver added a saxophone section and by 1927 sounded a lot like Henderson. Red Nichols built his famous Five Pennies up to a big band in 1926 and 1927. Even Louis Armstrong's Hot Five, once the quintessential dixieland group, was using arrangements by 1928.

But—and this is the critical point—if Americans wanted their jazz played by big bands, they continued to want it hot. Over the years between, say, 1926 and 1935, the hotter big bands gradually came to the fore, and the sweet bands lost ground bit by bit, until by the peak of the "swing band" boom in the years around 1940, it was the bands playing a lot of hot music that dominated. In the end it was not the bands of Whiteman, Specht, or Lopez that became the models for big-band jazz but the bands of Ellington, Goldkette, Bennie Moten, Ben Pollack, Nichols, McKinney's Cotton Pickers, Casa Loma, and most especially Fletcher Henderson. It was a two-stage process: first Grofé and Whiteman combined jazz rhythms with carefully worked-out arrangements to create symphonic jazz; then Henderson, Ellington, Goldkette, and the rest souped up the symphonic jazz with good jazz solos, stronger rhythm sections, and—most particularly—arranged passages that captured a true jazz feeling, to produce a music hotter than Whiteman would, or could, make it.

The smoother symphonic style by no means died out; a substantial proportion of the American public continued to relish it, and some sweet bands, like that of Guy Lombardo, remained highly popular right through the swing era and beyond. But the hot style slowly became dominant. By 1930 Duke Ellington was Victor's second-best seller.[40] The next year, he was so celebrated that he was asked to the White House to meet President Hoover as one of a group of leading American blacks.[41] In the same year the magazine *Orchestra World* placed him first, saying in a profile of Ellington, "At the age of 32, Ellington is one of the few recognized rulers in dance music, supreme in his field of the hot jungle tune. . . . Ellington's meteoric rise to fame is a flowering of the trend toward negro music in dance form so popular in America after the war."[42] As early as 1927 Whiteman himself recognized what was happening, and raided the Goldkette orchestra for its hot soloists, including Beiderbecke, and its primary arranger, Bill Challis. Roger Wolfe Kahn, leader of another popular dance band, added Bud Freeman to his orchestra to supply hot touches: "It was dance music, and I was just a soloist in the band," Freeman said, meaning that he did not play the written, ensemble parts.[43] Benny Goodman was being hired for dozens of recording sessions to add hot touches to dance-band and vocal recordings. By the last years of the 1920s, dance music had to have at least some good jazz ingredients to be successful. The New Orleans clarinetist Tony Parenti said, "Society band leaders like Meyer Davis and Joe Moss always wanted to have at least one good jazzman in their bands. . . . They wouldn't play jazz at those High social functions, of course, but they did want a man with them who could play a couple of solo choruses on the up-tempo things."[44]

The supporters of symphonic jazz were unhappy; in 1927 Henry Osborne Osgood noted that despite the success of symphonic jazz, "regrettably hot jazz is coming back,"[45] and as early as 1925 *Orchestra World* was "weary of the flood of hot stuff which is continually rushing in on us."[46] But there was no damming the flood. In 1931 the American correspondent for the English *Melody Maker* said that colleges "call for nothing but hot music."[47] In fact, the colleges had all along proven to be important bastions of jazz. The Original Dixieland Jass Band was playing colleges regularly by 1918; Bix Beiderbecke was playing fraternity dances at Northwestern and the University of Indiana by 1922. Very quickly, student jazz bands sprouted on American campuses: the Original Hot 5 of Harvard in 1924;[48] the Tulanians in 1925;[49] the Maroon Five at the University of Chicago, which Jimmy McPartland sometimes joined, in about 1925;[50] the Purple Pirates at Williams from 1925 or 1926; the Texas University Troubadors and the Yale Collegians from 1930. These were not ordinary dance bands but true jazz bands.[51] Some of them made commercial recordings which show them playing a very high level of jazz. Tom Howell, cornetist for the Texas University Troubadors, and the better-known Stew Pletcher, with the Yale group, were both first-rate jazz musicians, working in the Beiderbecke mold, and would have held their own with the best professionals of the time.

By the mid-1920s, students were routinely booking first-rate jazz bands for dances, according to Francis "Cork" O'Keefe, who was to become a major figure in the band business in the 1930s.

> I had the Five Pennies. I had all the college work with the small groups. Up at Williams they'd want six men. Can you get us Eddie Lang, can you get us this one, is Red Nichols available on trumpet? These kids were hep in those days. And the same at Princeton, all the other places. It was great for the fraternity dances . . . and the musicians would not only get paid, but they'd have a ball. At a fraternity house they'd be half-stewed by the time the dance was over. Some of them would have worked for nothing.[52]

Herb Sanford, later active in music, and author of a book on the Dorsey Brothers, said that in the 1920s, "Campuses were good territory for jazz musicians. The students understood and appreciated the music, and the musicians liked to play for them."[53] In 1927 *Variety* reported, "A feature of the season is the popularity of a colored orchestra for college proms. Fletcher Henderson's twelve-piece [band] is in demand, its 'hot' music catching the fancy of the college steppers."[54] That year Henderson played dances at Yale, Union, Dartmouth, Amherst, Brown, and Princeton.[55] A pinnacle of some kind was reached at a May 1929 Princeton house party which featured the bands of Fletcher Henderson, Duke Ellington, Luckey Roberts, Charlie Johnson, McKinney's Cotton Pickers, and Miff Mole's Molers— surely one of the greatest concentrations of jazz talent in history.[56]

By 1931 Armstrong, fronting a big band, "sold over 100,000 records . . . without the aid of ballyhoo,"[57] among them such masterpieces as his *Star Dust* and *Between the Devil and the Deep Blue Sea*. Fletcher Henderson's first real hit, which went on selling for ten years, was his *Sugarfoot Stomp* with Armstrong playing the blazing hot King Oliver solo.[58] Ellington's initial success was built on such hot numbers as *Black and Tan Fantasy*.[59]

In short, there can be no doubt of the popularity of hot jazz during this period. In 1928 *Variety* said,

> American interest in futuristic jazz is commercially manifested through the large sales of ultra-modernistic music as recorded by Boyd Senter, Bix Berderbecke [*sic*], Miff Mole, Red McKenzie, Ed Lang, Joe Venuti, Red Nichols, Frankie Trumbauer, and Condon's Chicagoans on Okeh disks. Their jazzique is of the extremely 'heated' variety and the sales turnover evidences how interested the American youth is in jazz music of this calibre. . . .[60]

Senter aside, all the names on the list are recognized today as major jazz figures of the period. (For whatever reasons, the list does not include any of the equally popular blacks, like Ellington and Henderson.)

If we are to understand how jazz relates to American culture, we must keep in mind that the audience for this hot big-band jazz, like the audience for the earlier dixieland, was mainly white, drawn from the mainstream of the culture. The white bands of Goldkette, Nichols, Pollack, Casa Loma, and others were playing, as ever, almost exclusively for white audiences in cabarets, dance halls, and theaters. So were the black bands: through the 1920s Henderson was working mainly at the segregated (for whites) Roseland dance hall and making summer tours through Pennsylvania, New England, and the midwest playing largely in white dance halls.[61] Ellington was mainly playing at the Kentucky Club, and then the Cotton Club—both restricted to whites, although they would admit a few black show-business stars.[62] Louis Armstrong first became widely known in 1924 and 1925 as the hot soloist with Henderson at Roseland; for the next few years he worked in black-and-tans on Chicago's South Side; by 1929 he was at a segregated club, Connie's Inn, in Harlem and was doubling in a Broadway show with a white audience.[63] Fats Waller was playing the same two locations at the same time. Earl Hines played black-and-tans in Chicago for many years after the mid-1920s. Speaking of one of these clubs, the Sunset, where he worked with Louis Armstrong, who was then coming to the first maturity of his powers, Hines said,

> . . . although the club was on the main stem of the Negro neighborhood, it drew whites as much as colored. Sometimes the audience was ninety percent white. Even the mixing of white girls and colored pimps seemed to be an attraction. People came in big parties from Chicago's Gold Coast to see these shows.[64]

Moreover, all of these great jazz musicians were broadcasting regularly from quite early in the decade. Both Kid Ory in Los Angeles and Bessie Smith in Atlanta made radio broadcasts as early as 1923.[65] Ethel Waters, with the Fletcher Henderson Jazz Masters, broadcast from New Orleans in 1921: "We were the first colored entertainers to broadcast from that station."[66] Fletcher Henderson was broadcasting with his own orchestra regularly from 1924 on,[67] and Duke Ellington also was, from about the same time. The audience for radio was probably ninety-percent white, and some of the bands were broadcasting at around six o'clock in the evening, supper time in the East and Midwest: the audience for those shows was made up of American families. Radio was intended for a mainstream audience, and the people who ran the industry were feeding that audience an enormous amount of the best hot jazz— among them pieces that, as recorded, are revered classics of the music. It is literally true that there was more good jazz broadcast in the United States in the 1920s than there is today, virtually all of it live. As early as 1924 there existed in Chicago a small station specializing in jazz, WBBM, run as a hobby, as many of these early small stations were.[68] John Hammond, American correspondent for the *Melody Maker*, wrote in 1932,

> English readers can have no idea of what American radio programs are like. There are, literally, hundreds of them, and most of them go on almost non-stop around the clock. So wide and varied is the list of stars available that it is almost possible to tune in on your favorite band or singer at any hour of the day or night.[69]

To be sure, the enormous output Hammond was speaking of was hardly all pure jazz; jazz constituted only a portion of it. But all the important jazz musicians of the time were broadcasting regularly. It will make today's jazz fans faint with envy to realize that in those days casual listeners were dancing in their living rooms to live solos by Johnny Hodges, Coleman Hawkins, Louis Armstrong, Jack Teagarden, Bix Beiderbecke, and dozens of others.

An important fact to emphasize is that many of these famous musicians did not begin, in the early 1920s, as jazz musicians. This was especially true of Ellington and Henderson, who eventually built what many critics would consider the most important jazz bands of the decade. Both men had come out of middle-class homes and grew up hearing neither jazz nor the blues. Both had for their first groups polite dance bands that played little jazz. Both turned their bands into jazz bands gradually in the years between 1923 and 1926 or so. My point is that both of these seminal groups *became* jazz bands while they were playing for white, mainstream audiences in cabarets, dance halls, theaters, over the radio, and on records.

I do not mean that blacks were cynically manufacturing a product to suit whites. Young musicians of both races were excited by the new jazz music, and wanted to play it as often as they could; they would no doubt have found ways to do so in any case. But they could not have made their livings at it had white audiences not been enamored of the music. The great jazz of the music's early classic period developed because millions of white Americans liked it, and would pay money to hear it.

The case of the Whiteman band and Bix Beiderbecke is informative. Among the myths of jazz it has frequently been said that Beiderbecke drank himself to death because he was buried in the Whiteman orchestra, unable to express his jazz feeling. As Marshall Stearns put it, "the frustration of being allowed to play so little, when he was hired because he could play so much, led to all kinds of personal problems."[70] In fact, Beiderbecke played solos, short or long, on thirty percent of the records he made with Whiteman. Some of these are considered masterpieces of the genre by critics today. It is reasonable to assume that on location, even more than in the recording studio, Whiteman allowed Bix to stretch out. Bix also played his famous piano composition *In A Mist* as a trio with pianists Roy Bargy and Lennie Hayton at Carnegie Hall in 1928.[71] Furthermore, besides Beiderbecke, at one time or another Whiteman was giving solo space to other important players, among them Frankie Trumbauer and Jimmy Dorsey. There was some kind of jazz soloing on half of Whiteman's records. I am not trying to make a case for Whiteman's band as a genuine jazz band; my point is simply that Paul Whiteman had a bulldog grasp on American taste, was leading far and away the most popular dance band in America at the time, and felt it prudent to give his audiences a considerable amount of jazz by the best white players he could buy.

The story from 1930 on is better known, and I need touch on it only lightly. In the early years of the 1930s jazz—at least the musicians who played it—suffered a setback, primarily because of the economic crisis of the Depression, which hurt the nightclubs, and because of radio, which "pretty well killed every other kind of entertainment," as Hammond wrote at the time.[72] But jazz continued to live, if in a somewhat reduced state. Contrary to statements by later writers, more than a thousand jazz sides were cut and issued in the early 1930s, among them some of the treasured classics of the music. The major big bands were never short of work: the Ellington, Casa Loma, and other groups worked steadily through the worst years of the Depression. Furthermore, the period saw a substantial growth in the jazz education movement in the United States, which has become so big a force in the music today. Warrick L. Carter, writing in *Jazz Educator's Journal*, says that "The true pioneer in jazz pedagogy within a school setting was Len Dowden, who first provided instruction in jazz in 1919,"[73] when he was a student teacher at Tuskegee Institute. By 1924, piano teachers were advertising lessons in jazz playing in *Billboard*.[74] However, the movement did not really develop for another ten or more years. According to Carter,

> During the 1930s, private teachers in Chicago, New York, Boston, Houston, Denver, and Los Angeles began establishing studios for the express purpose of teaching jazz improvisation. As early as 1935 Norbert Bleihoff wrote the first text attempting to explain techniques involving improvisation and arranging for the jazz ensemble.[75]

Then, in 1935, came the famous swing-band boom. The swing bands, which grew directly out of the models provided by Ellington, Casa Loma, Pollack, Goldkette, and especially Henderson, became the purveyors of American's popular music. In 1938, eighty-five percent of fifty million records issued were swing, and in 1939 Benny Goodman, broadcasting on the Camel Caravan show, drew two or three million people a night three nights a week.[76] The swing-band heroes were as celebrated as movie stars, their marriages and divorces chronicled in the gossip columns; many of them got rich. A 1936 *Down Beat* headline said, "Flesh and Blood Bands Break Records, Set New Money High."[77] The next year the New York City Board of Education announced plans to have weekly jazz lectures given in the city high schools by, among others, Goodman, Ellington, George Gershwin and Red Nichols.[78] In the same year *Variety* estimated that there were 150,000 juke boxes in the United States. The biggest juke-box hits of 1936 were Fats Waller's *I'm Going to Sit Right Down and Write Myself a Letter*, Casa Loma's *Casa Loma Stomp*, Armstrong's *Shoe Shine Boy*, Andy Kirk's *Until the Real Thing Comes Along*, two Goodman records, three Bing Crosby sides, and two sweet items.[79] The juke-box audience probably preferred a somewhat hotter music than the public as a whole, but the list is nonetheless some indication of American taste in popular music at the time.

The big swing bands were of course offering a good deal of ordinary pop material arranged for dancing, but the hot pieces were essential to the mix. By my own count, based on a careful listening to all of Benny Goodman's records during the formative years of swing in 1935–36, two-thirds were hot swing numbers, one-third slow ballads. Some of the biggest hits of the period were swingers, like Tommy Dorsey's *Boogie-Woogie*, Glenn Miller's *In the Mood*, Duke Ellington's *Take the A Train*, Count Basie's *One O'Clock Jump*, Benny Goodman's *King Porter Stomps*, Harry James's *Two O'Clock Jump*, and Charlie Barnet's *Cherokee*. Some bands, such as those of Sammy Kaye and Guy Lombardo, were very successful playing nothing but sweet music; but most had to base their music on jazz if they were to hold their audiences. The jitterbugs who sold out the Paramount Theatre when Benny Goodman appeared were not there for the sentimental tunes but to hear the band blast away at *Sing, Sing, Sing*.

Once again, although the black bands and occasionally the white ones played black dance halls and theaters, by far the largest part of the audience for the swing bands was white. The great soloists of the period, like Lester Young, Roy Eldridge, Johnny Hodges, Bunny Berigan, Benny Goodman, Charlie Christian, and dozens of others were developing their art, if we may term it that, mainly for mainstream whites. Some of the best jazz of the period, like the Goodman and Ellington small-group records, Coleman Hawkins's *Body and Soul*, and others, were hits, to one degree or another.

Also during the 1930s, the small jazz group regained its popularity. Beginning in about 1935, as Prohibition ended, nightclubs that featured small bands began to reopen on New York's Fifty-second Street, in Greenwich Village, and elsewhere across the United States. These groups were frequently led by some of the finest musicians of the period.[80] Once again, it was primarily whites who provided the audience at the Famous Door, Cafe Society, and similar places.

The swing movement collapsed after World War II, but the period that followed was, if anything, better for jazz. Through the late 1940s and the 1950s, especially with the development of the college jazz concert and later the jazz festival, a number of jazz musicians became wealthy, and dozens more were able to make comfortable livings. Miles Davis, Dave Brubeck, Louis Armstrong, Duke Ellington, and Count Basie at various times had gross incomes in the hundreds of thousands, and in some cases millions, of dollars annually. In the late 1940s Lester Young could make $50,000 a year,[81] and even John Coltrane, playing a good deal of tough avant-garde music, could make a quarter of a million dollars a year before his death in the 1960s.[82] In 1953 *Down Beat* reported,

Jazz is big business today. It's an important and money-making part of every major record company's activities and a major part of most minor firms' work. The jazz clubs flourish all over the country. . . . What today's kids want is jazz.[83]

Again, this audience was largely white. The black novelist Ralph Ellison later wrote, ". . . interestingly enough, Bird [Charlie Parker] was indeed a 'white hero.' His greatest significance was for the educated white middle-class youth whose reactions to the inconsistencies of American life was the stance of casting off its education, language, dress, manners, and moral standards. . . ." And he went on to quote the black jazz drummer Art Blakey as saying of blacks, "They never heard of [Bird]."[84]

Jazz suffered a second slump in the mid- to late 1960s and early 1970s in face of the tremendous rock boom, but in the years since it has regained much of the lost ground. The record stores are filled with jazz records, both reissues and new pieces by young stars; local, state, and national governments and private universities and foundations are supporting jazz in one form or another to the extent of millions of dollars worth of grants and scholarships; books on jazz, many of them published by European firms eager to cash in on the American market, flood the bookstores. Hundreds of colleges and thousands of high schools offer jazz courses and jazz training ensembles. New York, which was down to six jazz clubs in the late 1960s, now has at least twenty. Jazz is probably not as broadly popular in America today as it was in the 1920s when Bix Beiderbecke was the principal soloist in the country's most successful dance orchestra, or the swing period of 1935–40, when Duke Ellington was playing his thorny *Ko-ko* for audiences in places like Fargo, North Dakota; but it has a substantial following nonetheless. A recent study commissioned by the National Jazz Service Organization found that some sixteen million Americans had attended jazz events in the previous year, and that "nearly one-third of the adult population" of the country listened to jazz at least occasionally, mainly on records.[85]

It will be argued that these tens of millions of Americans are not serious jazz listeners, nor very knowledgeable about the music. But that is precisely the point: there exists in the United States a huge body of casual jazz fans, who enjoy the music to a point, or like particular players or styles of playing, and will occasionally go out to a jazz concert, tune into a jazz program, or buy a jazz record or two. These millions of casual jazz fans take jazz for granted, as something that is in the American air, something they have always been aware of. Europeans, even those who know the American situation fairly well, have little idea of how much jazz activity goes on in the United States. In addition to the celebrated professional groups, there are, scattered across the country, literally hundreds of informally organized jazz bands which play in public regularly, sometimes for very good fees. Some of these are quite rough and untutored, but others are staffed by professionals and first-rate semi-professionals, and play jazz at a high level. It is quite common for Americans to hire such bands to play at store openings, art exhibitions, weddings, college re-unions,and similar occasions. Americans are simply used to hearing jazz in one style or another at celebrations, and think little of it. Indeed, when we add to these in-formal jazz bands the thousands of training orchestras in colleges and schools, we can calculate that millions of Americans have had the experience of playing—or at least attempting to play—jazz. There are more competent jazz *players* in the United States than there are fans in some entire European nations. And it is the existence of these players and of the millions of casual fans which, more than anything, demonstrates how thoroughly jazz is woven into the American culture.

Even if we discount the casual listeners, there remains a substantial, if much smaller, body of Americans who take the music seriously, and make it a major part of their lives. It is difficult to guess how large this group is, but estimating from attendance at the big jazz festivals, which can run to 100,000, and nightly attendance at jazz clubs, which on a good night could be 20,000, we can judge that the number of serious jazz fans in the United States must be counted in the tens of thousands, far more than would be found elsewhere.

Given all of this, how has it been possible for jazz writers, virtually without excep-tion, to have insisted that the music has been neglected or actively despised in its native land? I will attempt to answer that question shortly; but first we must at-tend to the second of the great myths of jazz, that it was first appreciated as an art for Europeans.

III

Writers for *Melody Maker*, an English trade paper for dance-band musicians, were beginning to write with some, if incomplete, comprehension of white jazz musicians by 1927, and by 1930 they were coming to appreciate the black players as well. In the same year, Hugues Panassié in Paris began to write about American jazz, once again with incomplete understanding, for a new periodical called *Jazz Tango*. In 1934 he published his book *Le jazz hot*, and in 1935 he and some others started what they claimed to be the first significant periodical entirely devoted to jazz, *Jazz Hot*. Because many of the articles in the magazine were published in both French and English, it could be read by virtually every educated person in Europe and North America, and it became quite influential, especially among Europeans. Was there any comparable writing being done by Americans before the appearance of this European jazz criticism, if we may term it that; or is it in fact true that Europeans had to teach Americans the virtues of their own music?

Let us look at the evidence. To begin with, the "Negro question," as it was called in an earlier time, had long been a matter of vast concern to American scholars and social thinkers, as well as a good many ordinary citizens, who saw perfectly clearly that, leaving aside points of fairness and morality, racial friction was a cause of much unhappiness in American society. In the years between 1905 and 1914, when jazz was coming into being, American magazines carried over 600 articles on blacks and the problems associated with race, by my own count. Among them was a scattering of articles on "Negro music," which had long been of interest not only to musicologists, who treated it as they treated other native folk musics, but to the general public. In the nineteenth century a number of visitors to the South, including some Civil War officers, reported on black music, and eventually transcribed a number of songs and published them. Then in 1914, Henry Edward Krehbiel published his seminal *Afro-American Folksong*, which remains one of the best analyses of early black music.[1] By 1900 westernized black music, such as the so-called plantation songs and the spirituals, had been part of the American songbag for decades. Black music has continued to inflect American vernacular music ever since. The composer Virgil Thomson wrote as early as 1925, "Africa has made profound alterations in our European inheritance."[2] Americans took this "African" influence for granted; again and again, in newspaper pieces and magazine articles about jazz in the 1920s, the black roots of jazz were alluded to. The *Journal of*

American Folklore carried pieces on black music before there was any such thing as jazz, among them a well-known report by the anthropologist Charles Peabody, of the Peabody Museum of Harvard, on a curious music he had heard while on a dig in Mississippi, which is undoubtedly the first published comment on the blues. It was, Peabody said, "weird in interval and strange in rhythm."[3] Thus there was, in America, an intellectual basis for an interest in and analysis of black musical forms predating jazz.

When, then, did a serious appreciation of jazz first appear in the United States? Distinguishing between "serious appreciation" and simple popular acceptance is not easy: at what point does enthusiastic discussion pass over into criticism and analysis? Further, American and European intellectual traditions are somewhat different: Americans do not generally perceive among themselves a specific intellectual class, as Europeans do. Again, pragmatic American scholars have always tended to be somewhat wary of the theory-spinning which is at the heart of European intellectuality; they are more likely to value hard facts, and to let theory take care of itself. American intellectual interest in jazz therefore manifested itself somewhat differently at home from abroad, and those looking for "appreciation" of jazz in America would find less theorizing, and more practical analysis, than they would in Europe.

In any case, there was a considerable amount of serious appreciation of jazz right from the beginning. The first serious jazz lovers were the scores, eventually thousands, of young musicians, many of them still in adolescence, who were attracted to the music, especially after the success of the Original Dixieland Jass Band in 1917. As memoirs of these jazz pioneers show, they were intensely interested in the music, hoped to devote their lives to it, and quickly began to understand how it worked.[4] They swiftly shifted allegiance from the Original Dixieland Jass Band to better groups, like the Oliver Creole Jazz Band, the New Orleans Rhythm Kings, and eventually the Armstrong Hot Five.

These musicians were surrounded by a cluster of jazz fans, the size of which is difficult to determine, but which grew throughout the 1920s. It is clear that a considerable proportion of these fans were college and high-school students. R. D. Darrell, writing in 1932, said, "Hot jazz is less the concern of the public than of professional jazz musicians and a small but passionate amateur group of connoisseurs. . . . Mostly school or college boys, they hold a stage door Johnny reverence for their hot gods, talk for hours in semi-technical, near unintelligible lingo."[5] This college interest dates back to the early 1920s, when students began forming their own jazz bands, and has continued through to the present.

But it was not just students: there were many serious jazz fans scattered through the population at large, and certainly the roughly twelve million blacks in the country had their share. It is impossible to know how many people this totalled, but we can at least get some idea of the order of magnitude.

According to John Hammond, in 1930 New Haven record stores sold 300 of Louis Armstrong's discs to Yale students, and "the same was true in other college towns."[6] Hammond tended to be fairly casual about facts of this kind; but if we assume that the figure is approximately correct; subtract from it a large number of people who might have bought more than one Armstrong record; subract another number of people who might have had little interest in jazz but bought a record for the song Armstrong sang; and add a substantial number of people who were serious jazz listeners but bought no Armstrong records; we might fairly estimate that there were at least 200 serious jazz listeners in the Yale student population—both undergraduate and graduate—of roughly 5300.[7] Extrapolating this figure across an American college and university population of about 1.1 million,[8] we get a figure of 27,000 serious jazz listeners on American college campuses. If we assume that other Americans were far less interested in jazz than students were—by, let us say, a factor of ten— we arrive at a figure of roughly 300,000 serious jazz listeners in the United States in 1930, a figure which jibes with a guess by *Time* magazine in 1938 of a half-million "serious jazz fanciers" in the United States.[9]

This figure is of course only suggestive. But it does indicate that serious interest in jazz at the end of the 1920s, when the Europeans were first becoming aware of the music, was not confined to a tiny cult but was manifest in a substantial number of people, to whom must be added the casual listeners, who enjoyed the music in a more offhand way, numbering in the millions.

But it was not all just fan enthusiasm. Contrary to what is universally believed, there was good, serious writing about jazz from the beginning. The first analysis of jazz that I have been able to discover was made in 1917 by a Columbia University English professor, William Morrison Patterson. He had recently published a study of the rhythms of prose—it had been his doctoral dissertation—and he was quoted on jazz in the *Literary Digest*. His analysis of jazz rhythm, in which he says that it is based on a musician's "progressive retarding and acceleration guided by his sense of 'swing' . . .," was one of the best for decades.[10] To put this in perspective, we must remember that in 1917 both Louis Armstrong and Duke Ellington were musical apprentices attempting to learn the new music; at that point this college professor knew more about jazz than Ellington did.

Jazz, of course, was only beginning to make itself known in 1917, and serious writing on it was at first only a trickle. There was a piece on jazz in *The Review*, "A weekly journal of political and general discussion," in 1919;[11] a piece in *The Nation* in 1922; another in *The Dial* in 1923; and pieces in the *New York Times* Sunday magazine and entertainment section in 1919, 1921, and 1922. Some of this writing was discerning, some of it was not. One of the better articles was one by Carl Engel in *The Atlantic* in 1922, which said:

> . . . Jazz finds its last and supreme glory in the skill for improvisation exhibited by the performers. The deliberately scored jazz tunes are generally clumsy, pedestrian. . . . Jazz is abandon, is whimsicality in music. . . . Each player must be a clever musician, an originator as well as an interpreter. . . . The playing and writing down of jazz are two different things. When a jazz tune is written on paper, for a piano solo, it loses nine tenths of its flavor.[12]

For several years after about 1922, serious jazz writing was almost totally concerned with the symphonic version of Whiteman and others. Typical was a two-part series on "The Jazz Problem" in *The Etude* in 1924.[13] The magazine was fundamentally anti-jazz in attitude but felt it had to confront the issue. It did so by soliciting comments from various notables, including the composer John Alden Carpenter, Dr. Frank Damrosch, John Philip Sousa, Paul Specht, Leopold Stokowski, and the well-known rabbi Stephen Wise. Most of these celebrated people approved of jazz to one degree or another, but it was the symphonic version they were talking about. This attitude would prevail in jazz writing in popular magazines for two or three more years.

But not all serious critics of the music were wooed away by symphonic jazz. A lot of them believed that the Whiteman version of jazz lacked something that the original stuff had. Whiteman had opened his Aeolian Hall concert with a dixieland version of *Livery Stable Blues*, the Original Dixieland Jass Band's first hit. His intention was to contrast this "crude" older music unfavorably with the slicker work to follow on the program. He was made exceedingly uneasy when the audience cheered *Livery Stable Blues* lustily, although in the end the reception to the arranged pieces left him feeling justified. Olin Downes, of the *New York Times*, came out flatly in support of the dixieland form. He said,

> . . . Livery Stable Blues was introduced apologetically as an example of the depraved past from which modern jazz has risen. The apology is herewith indignantly rejected, for this is a glorious piece of impudence much better in its unbuttoned jocosity and Rabelasian laughter than other and more polite compositions that came later.[14]

He went on to point out that the American Negro "contributed fundamentally to this art, which can neither be frowned nor sneered away."

Virgil Thomson, becoming one of the country's most important composers and critics, felt the same. In *Vanity Fair*, a flossy magazine on the order of today's *New Yorker*, Thomson wrote that Whiteman

> . . . has refined [jazz,] smoothed its harshness, taught elegance to its rhythms, blended its jarring polyphonies into an ensemble of mellow harmonic unity. . . . He has suppressed what was striking and original in it, and taught it the manners of Vienna.[15]

As the popularity of the hotter music began to grow again, there was being produced in the United States the beginnings of a true jazz criticism. In September 1926 the Sunday *New York Times Magazine* ran a long, perceptive piece on the blues which included a quite accurate discussion of their origins. The author said,

> Blues in the original form are vanishing, but their influence has wrought a revolution in jazz and the moans of mad horns and the wails of demonic saxophones have caught the country's ear until the intelligentsia debate their worth; sponsors of the blues produce erudite anthologies, and sober psychologists ponder the social significance.[16]

In the same year, another excellent piece on the blues appeared in the *New Republic*. It was written by Abbe Niles, a folklorist, and said in part:

> The melody would be a four-bar phrase favoring a syncopated jugglery of a very few notes; the second phrase would vary somewhat the first, suggesting to the musical ear an excursion into the sub-dominant; the third would give a final version. Play between the keynote and its third was particularly frequent, and the tonic third characteristically coincides with the antepenultimate syllable of the line. And in these, as in other Negro songs, the singer was apt, in dealing with this particular note, to slur from flat to natural or vice versa.[17]

Then, speaking of W. C. Handy's attempts to write commercial versions of the blues, Niles said,

> In writing down this music, he chose to represent the primitive treatment of the tonic third, in some cases by the minor, simple, sometimes by introducing the minor third as a grace note to the major, or vice versa. . . . The more blue notes the "meaner" the blues. . . . In many blues there is not only strangeness, but beauty. . . . It may be a softly wistful beauty, or it may be the beauty of a savage and bitter power.[18]

This was a first-rate analysis: Niles both understood the blues technically and "appreciated" them.

Other pieces on jazz appeared in the *Literary Digest*, the *American Mercury*, and other such magazines.[19] In 1930 Charles Edward Smith, who was to become one of the better-known jazz writers of the period, produced a long discussion of jazz for the highbrow *Symposium*, in which he discussed virtually all of the major figures in jazz of the time and used the term "art" in reference to various jazz works. Armstrong's Hot Seven, Smith said, was the "most important band in jazz today," though he felt that Armstrong, "at present the only outstanding figure in jazz, succumbs more and more to the white man's notion of Harlem jazz.[20] This was the first in a long line of similar criticisms which would be made about Armstrong.

But the best American jazz criticism of the day was being done by three other men. The earliest of these to write good criticism was Carl Van Vechten. He is most famous for a very bad novel called *Nigger Heaven*, which has been used as an example of white confusion about black life, and he has been maligned in jazz history, in part due to attacks on him by John Hammond, who referred to his work as "drivel."[21] In fact, Van Vechten had a real knowledge of and genuine interest in blacks. His father had been co-founder of the Piney Woods School for black children, and he grew up in intimate contact with them. When he came to New York he was introduced to Harlem, then bubbling with the intellectual ferment of the Harlem Renaissance, by Walter White, later to be a major black leader. He developed a serious interest in black show business before almost any other white, and eventually asked Bessie Smith to his house to sing for his guests, and again to sit for a photographic portrait. He also became close to Ethel Waters. Van Vechten was immersed in the black world, and whatever his shortcomings as a novelist, he knew a great deal about black show business. His interest was in black music generally, rather than specifically in jazz, but he spent hundreds of hours in Harlem cabarets, during the 1920s, and he understood the music.[22]

In 1925 Van Vechten published three pieces on black show business in *Vanity Fair*—on Negro folk songs, the blues, and the black theater. They were literate, serious, and thoroughly informed. He said, for instance, of the blues:

> Like the Spirituals, the Blues are folk songs and are conceived in the same pentatonic scale, omitting the fourth and seventh tones—although these that have achieved publication or performance under sophisticated auspices have generally passed through a process of transmutation. . . . The music of the Blues has a peculiar language of its own, wreathed in melancholy ornament. It wails, this music, and limps languidly;

the rhythm is angular, like the sporadic skidding of an automobile on a wet pavement. . . . The words, however, in beauty and imaginative significance, far transcend in their crude poetic importance the words of the religious songs. They are eloquent with rich idioms, metaphoric phrases and striking word combinations.[23]

And, "To hear Clara Smith sing [*Any Woman's Blues*] is an experience that no one, who has had the privilege, will soon forget. Her voice, choking with moaning quarter tones, clutches the heart."[24] He quoted the black poet Langston Hughes: "There seems to be a monotonous melancholy, an animal sadness, running through all Negro jazz that is almost terrible at times;" and he concluded that the blues "deserve, therefore, from every point of view, the same serious attention that has tardily been awarded to the spirituals."[25]

One point that has to be kept in mind when examining this very early American writing on jazz is that the critics were dealing with jazz in the first stages of its development. The music was still dixieland played by relatively anonymous musicians in bands all playing in similar ways. When Van Vechten was writing for *Vanity Fair*, the idea of the jazz solo was only beginning to be developed, and Beiderbecke, Armstrong, Ellington, Henderson, Morton, and others had not yet made their significant recordings. As a consequence, this early criticism lacks the particularity that would come as the giants of the 1926–29 flowering emerged as individuals. It was, nonetheless, serious and informed writing.

The second of the three major American early-jazz critics came to jazz writing as the flowering was taking place. This was Robert Donaldson Darrell, who wrote for a magazine called *Phonograph Monthly Review*, which began in 1926 and died early in the Depression. The magazine is virtually unknown to jazz writers, and Darrell is even less well known, but it is my belief that he can make a fair claim to be called the first jazz critic. He was by no means the first to grasp the essence of jazz; in fact, he was relatively late in coming to the music. But he was the first person to review jazz regularly with sensitivity and perception, and he did so for some five years. The bulk of Darrell's critical judgments from about mid-1927 on hold up today. The same could be said of very few critics of the period, in any field.

Darrell was a Bostonian who studied classical music at the New England Conservatory. He eventually decided he would never be another Beethoven, and turned to music criticism for a career. He belonged to an intellectual circle which included R. P. Blackmur, who was to become one of the country's leading literary critics (Darrell's correspondence with Blackmur has been published), and in 1926 he was asked to work for *Phonograph Monthly Review*. This was a shoestring operation, and Darrell would eventually write a large portion of the magazine himself; but it was the first American consumer magazine devoted to records.[26]

Darrell initially had little interest in jazz, but he began reviewing popular records for the sake of completeness. "I was primarily the classical record reviewer, but then I had to take on these other records." His knowledge of popular music was small, and furthermore the magazine was headquartered in Boston, away from the primary scenes of jazz activity, Chicago and New York. He was simply opening boxes of review copies sent to him by the record companies, and going by what his ear told him.

> The first two or three months there I didn't pay any particular attention. Then all of a sudden a couple of the Red Nichols records, and particularly the Ellington *Black and Tan Fantasy*, really snapped me to attention. The reason why I was so taken with Ellington—one of the reasons—was [that he] struck me as an orchestrator in the class of Ravel, Respighi, and Strauss. It was the serious element in it that got me at first, although with the Red Nichols thing it was the dry, ironic jazz wit. That was something brand new to me.

Darrell's taste, flawed at first, quickly grew better. In the first issue of the magazine, in 1926, he said of jazz, "When it is good, it is good music and worthy of careful consideration and study,"[27] and in that issue he listed as of interest records by Armstrong's Hot Five, the Original Memphis Five, and the Henderson and Goldkette orchestras. His grasp of jazz, however, did not begin to become firm until the middle of the next year. In May of 1927 he praised a record by Mole's Molers, but found the Beiderbecke classic *Singing the Blues* "rather disappointing."[28] Then, about June, he came across Ellington's *Black and Tan Fantasy*. At first he found the growl effects funny, and played the record for the amusement of his friends. But very quickly he began to feel that there was something else there. He became an ardent supporter of Ellington, reviewing his records in almost every issue, and went on to develop into a fine, discerning jazz critic. In July 1927 he ran a long overview of American music in which he said, "Many of the blues are merely popular songs sung in blues style, but the real thing is of authentic quality, unparalleled by anything else in musical literature," and went on to say,

> In the number of works which have recently appeared on the subject of jazz, the part Negro music has played in its genesis has been debated at length; it is sufficient here to say that the jazz of today has succeeded in assimilating whatever Negro, minstrel, semi-folk music, or other influences which went to make it up, and it is now a distinct musical form—American to the core. Various European attempts to create or even play ragtime or jazz . . . all fail to catch the essential American spirit.[29]

In these first years of his criticism Darrell was dividing jazz into black and white schools. In September 1927, in a wrap-up on jazz for the *Review* he said, "The principal exponent of 'hot' jazz is the white orchestra under the direction of Red Nichols." The leading black orchestras on his list were Ellington, Henderson, and Oliver, and "for extreme forms of 'hot' jazz, which return again to the 'noisy' side—Louis Armstrong's Seven."[30]

Darrell was not yet quite on the mark: today we would put Armstrong in a class of his own during that period, well above Red Nichols, although in fact Nichols's work is far better than later writers have said. But Darrell's sense of what was good jazz became surer and surer over the succeeding months; in 1929 and 1930 he was singling out Ellington and Armstrong for the highest praise. Ellington's *Blues I Love to Sing* and *Creole Love Call* were "among the greatest hot performances of all times."[31] He said, "Ring Dem Bells will strike joy to the heart of the hot jazzist, an incredibly skillful and lighthearted performance, embellished by natty wa-wa dialogue and joyous rhythmic bell work, although fit to rank with the best Ellington records of the past—which is lively praise indeed."[32] He wrote,

> The marvelously gifted (jazzically) pianist of Louis Armstrong's orchestra [Earl Hines] gets only an occasional opportunity to display his talents in solo discs, so connoisseurs of ultra-modern jazz should not let his present coupling of original Caution Blues and A Monday Date slip by. The former is moderately interesting, but the intently rambling Monday Date decidedly extraordinary. Strawinskites and Bartokians will find more than a trace of their cherished modern feeling right here. . . .[33]

He said that Armstrong's *Dear Old Southland* duet with pianist Buck Washington, "with it's introductory exhortation and its lugubrious reminiscences of Deep River, is a most remarkable piece, pervaded by a singular and extremely intense feeling, wracking struggle for untrammelled expression that is a very far cry indeed from the slick sophistication and self-confidence of most jazz."[34] Ellington's *Echoes of the Jungle* was "a disc that will amaze even those who are familiar with the Duke's achievements in the past. The elaborate texture and diabolically ingenious arrangements will astound even the students of such modern orchestrators as Ravel and Strawinsky."[35] Ellington's *Creole Love Call, Ring Dem Bells,* and *Echoes of the Jungle*; Hines's *A Monday Date*; and Armstrong's *Dear Old Southland* are today among the most treasured records from the period. Along the way Darrell praised Bennie Moten, King Oliver, Red Allen, McKinney's Cotton Pickers, Jelly Roll Morton, Bix Beiderbecke, Benny Goodman, Red Nichols, Joe Venuti—virtually the whole roster of important jazz musicians of the day.

38

By 1931 Darrell was putting reviews of the best jazz of the time into a section of their own. His knowledge was considerable and his taste sure:

> For all the fact that *Ellington* has become too popular and too busy to do his best work at all times, the Duke still has an occasional disc up his sleeve that is not only quite unbeatable, but is a genuine musical (not mere jazzical) achievement. His *Jungle Band*'s coupling of Dreamy Blues and Runnin' Wild, on Brunswick 4952, is one of these works. Runnin' Wild is one of the finest dance tunes ever written (as Gilbert Seldes and many another has testified) and Ellington's version is done with an abandon as magnificent as that of the music itself. But the Dreamy Blues, one of Ellington's own compositions, is the real musical achievement. It is a poignantly restrained and nostalgic piece with glorious melodic endowment and scoring that even Ravel and Strawinsky might envy. Indeed it actually recalls those hushed muted trumpets of the beginning of the second part of the "Rite of Spring." The very same piece is played again under the name Mood Indigo by the *Harlem Footwarmers* on Okeh 8840. Despite the change of name in both title and orchestra, the performance sounds exactly the same, although the Okeh recording is less brilliant, departing somewhat from the splendid authenticity of tone color reproduction in the Brunswick disc, but possibly adding a little to the restrained atmospheric qualities of the piece. The coupling here [*Sweet Chariot*] is a lugubrious slow, bewailing piece of considerable interest (it is also by Ellington), but by no means as striking as the Mood Indigo, alias Dreamy Blues. Is Ellington's band also the *Harlem Music Masters*? Their performance of Ring Dem Bells (Okeh 41468) is very closely akin to that of Ellington in his splendid Victor version of the same piece. Again the jaunty flow, fine coloring and wa-wa work calls for emphatic phrase [*sic*]. (The coupling is provided by *Louis Armstrong* and his *Sebastian New Cotton Club Orchestra* in a version of Body and Soul that contrasts refreshingly with the average performances, and which is played and sung with far more genuine feeling and force.) Ellington's current Victor disc (23022) is one of his virtuoso feats. Old Man Blues is a grand rollicking tune, played to a standstill by the entire band, with Duke's piano well ahead. Jungle Nights in Harlem contains some more amazing piano and orchestral effects (Rimsky-Korsakow would rub his ears on hearing some of the tone colors here!). Note the parabolic flights in particular. Fantastic music, astoundingly played.[36]

Perhaps most impressive is his assessment of *Creole Rhapsody*, a two-sided piece which was the first of Ellington's attempts to write symphonic jazz, as "not in the finest Ellington tradition."[37] Darrell immediately felt that this first example of Ellington's penchant for fancier forms was a mistake, a judgment many critics have agreed with since.

Darrell's best writing about jazz came at the very end of his career in the field, with two long pieces in *Disques* for June and September 1932. The one on Ellington, inevitably, was particularly fine. It reads in part:

Out of the vast bulk of [Ellington's] work, thrown off in his cabaret-dance-hall-vaudeville recording routine, I found a goodly residue of music that was of the same or superior calibre as [*Black and Tan Fantasy*]; and disregarding all that was merely conventional, noisy, and cheap, there was still a quintessence of precious quality for which one has no apter term than genius. . . . As a purveyor and composer of music that must be danced to (if he is to earn his living), Ellington's composition is narrowly limited by dance exigencies, while he is allowed a wide range of expression in the way of instrumentation and performance. It is hardly remarkable that the latter experimentation has borne fruit; what is remarkable is that working within constricted walls he has yet been able to give rein to his creative imagination and racial urge for expression. Perhaps the very handicaps, permitting no high-flown excursions into Negro Rhapsodies and tone poems, allowing no escape from the fundamental beat of dance rhythm, have enabled Ellington to concentrate his musical virility, draw out its full juice, dissipating none of his forces in vain heaven-storming. . . . Ellington's compositions gravitate naturally toward two types, the strong rhythmed pure dance pieces (*Birmingham Breakdown, Jubilee Stomp, New Orleans Low Down, Stevedore Stomp*, etc.), or the slower paced lyrical pieces with a less forcefully rhythmed dance bass (*Mood Indigo, Take It Easy, Awful Sad, Mystery Song*, etc.). Occasionally the two are combined with tremendous effectiveness, as in the *East St. Louis Toodle-O, Old Man Blues*, or *Rocking in Rhythm*. The most striking characteristic of all his works, and the one which stamps them ineradicably as his own, is the individuality and unity of style that weld composition, orchestration, and performance into one inseparable whole. . . . Harmonically Ellington is apt and subtle rather than obvious or striking. Except for sheerly declamatory lines, his melodies are clothed on the harmonies they themselves suggest. He thinks not in chordal blocks, but in moving parts. . . . In exploitation of new tonal coloring, as has already been suggested, Ellington has proceeded further than any composer—popular or serious—of today. His command of color contrast and blend approaches at times an art of polytimbres.[38]

Darrell's *Disques* article is one of the finest pieces of writing that has ever been done on Ellington, and it was written while Ellington himself was still finding his voice. Darrell was dead on the mark when he pointed out Ellington's genius with tone coloring and his approach to harmony, and especially when he sensed that Ellington was successful *because* he eschewed "Negro Rhapsodies and tone poems"; in my view, it was after Ellington had been encouraged to compose precisely those sorts of composition—at first by the Englishmen Lambert and Hughes—that his work began to falter.

It should be pointed out that R. D. Darrell is coming to be recognized as one of America's important music critics of this century. The musicologist Carol J. Oja has recently said that "when the history of music criticism in this country is finally written, he will figure prominently as one of our first major record critics and as someone who, in the 1920s and '30s, championed a number of American composers before it was fashionable to do so."[39] Darrell was in any case, writing better about jazz in 1932 than anyone else, anywhere—among other things, he understood music technically—and he makes a useful benchmark to tell us how far serious appreciation of jazz in the United States had developed by this time: although he was writing better than anybody else I have been able to discover, he was certainly far from the first American to take jazz seriously, and he was, operating from Boston, not the most knowledgeable student of the subject either. There were, by this time in the United States, thousands of people who understood jazz as well as Darrell, although no one could write about it with such skill.

Darrell left *Phonograph Monthly Review* as of the November 1931 issue, but continued to write for it on a part-time basis. The magazine folded a few months later, a victim of the Depression, leaving him to cap his career as a jazz critic with the *Disques* pieces. He was eager to write a book about Ellington, whom he interviewed in 1932, which would combine biography with musical analysis and a discography.[40] Unfortunately Ellington would not cooperate, but Darrell did put together a discography of Ellington which was published with the *Disques* piece—the first published jazz discography that I am aware of.

The third of our forgotten jazz critics from the period was Abbe Niles. From February 1928 to January 1929 he wrote monthly music reviews for *The Bookman*, a highbrow weekly covering intellectual topics, mainly literary. Niles was primarily concerned with folk music, but he gradually became interested in jazz, and by about the middle of 1928 he began to separate the better jazz records from ordinary dance music. Like Darrell's, his taste became surer with time, and by the January 1929 issue of *The Bookman*, in which he published a year-end roundup of jazz, he called Ellington "supreme in his field" and gave special mention to Red Nichols, Joe Venuti's Blue Four, Frankie Trumbauer, Clarence Williams, Armstrong's *West End Blues*, Bessie Smith, and others. It is true that he also gave Whiteman high praise, but his perceptions were, in terms of today's critical views, about seventy-five percent correct.

We must not exaggerate the extent of this early jazz criticism. Compared with the published writing about classical music, it was very small indeed, amounting to not more than a score of magazine and newspaper articles at best, in addition to the reviews by Darrell and Niles. Even Darrell was devoting far more space to classical-music records in his magazine than to jazz. Yet it is clear that there existed in the United States by the middle years of the 1920s a sense among intellectuals that jazz ought to be taken seriously. In Niles, Darrell, Van Vechten, Charles

Edward Smith, and some others, the country had a cadre of knowledgeable and literate jazz critics, some of them with considerable musical training. Highbrow magazines were opening their pages to serious discussions of jazz, and the big popular magazines continued to run dozens of articles, good and bad, on jazz through this period. In 1925 no less a personage than Edmund Wilson, soon to become dean of American letters, could call the jazz dancer Johnny Hudgins, then at the Club Alabam in Times Square, "a remarkable artist," in the pages of the *New Republic*.[41]

Furthermore, this critical writing, however limited, makes it clear that jazz had the support of important members of what can be called the serious-music establishment. Rob Darrell was editor of a magazine devoted largely to erudite discussion of Brahms and Beethoven; Carl Engel was a composer and head of the Music Division of the Library of Congress; Carl Van Vechten was writing on music and dance for the *Musical Quarterly* and *Bellman*; Olin Downes was the classical-music critic of the *New York Times*; Virgil Thomson was an important composer and critic. These were not hot-eyed youths out to *épater les bourgeois* but men with solid training in music, in positions to influence public taste. They all understood the difference between symphonic jazz and the hotter version, and all went on record as preferring the latter.

In any case, no matter how many serious listeners there were in the United States, and how small the body of jazz criticism there was in the 1920s, nothing even remotely like it existed anywhere else in the world at that time. No periodical of any kind anywhere else printed anything on jazz that was the equal of the work that Van Vechten, Darrell, and the others were doing in the second half of the 1920s. European national periodicals would not give jazz attention for years after American ones did, and jazz records, even into the 1930s, typically sold no more than 1,500 copies even in Great Britain, where the audience for jazz was largest.[42] The European jazz public numbered in the hundreds.[43] At a time when at least a few people in America were reviewing recordings by Armstrong, Ellington, Morton and others as they were coming out, these names were known in Europe, if at all, to only a tiny handful of people even among musicians. What, then, was the jazz situation in Europe?

IV

A few Europeans were aware of the Original Dixieland Jass Band records when they began coming out in 1917, and in 1919 a promoter brought the group to England. The press was uniformly uncomprehending and unhappy with the music, and they suggested that audiences were, too. One reviewer said, "Most are obviously bewildered by the weird discords, but some, to judge by the cynical smiles, evidently think that it is a musical joke that is hardly worthwhile attempting."[1] Many years later, in a retrospective piece, the *Melody Maker* said flatly that the group "was a complete flop at the Palladium. Nobody understood it."[2] The band's appearance produced no little swirls of imitators, and was generally forgotten after it left.

In the years thereafter, a number of American dance-band musicians came to Europe, where they were in high demand and could command good salaries. Local musicians were exceedingly unhappy about this influx.[3] American musicians were ordered out of France in 1924,[4] at least one was deported from England,[5] and the Germans also tried to get rid of them.[6] English musicians, after a decade of battling, finally were able in 1935 to institute a ban on American bands which lasted until after World War II. Europeans were thus deliberately closing the doors on the American musicians who could have taught them the new hot music, although some did work sporadically in Europe especially in London and Paris, during the 1920s.

Some complete ensembles made tours as well: the Hickman group was in London in 1920 and 1921; Specht, Whiteman, and others came later. These, of course, were symphonic-jazz bands, but a few true jazz bands also made sporadic visits to Europe. Sidney Bechet was in England and France for periods in the 1920s, with Peyton's Six Jazz Kings and free-lancing; Mitchell's Jazz Kings played in Europe for a few years after World War I; Frank Guarente, Specht's hot trumpet star, was around for a while; an American group under pianist Billy Arnold toured in the early 1920s; and there were, at various periods, three or four other American groups, now mainly forgotten, playing at one time or another for dancing or in cabarets.[7]

But the sum total of this jazz activity in Europe was small. Bechet was deported from England and spent time in a French jail for his part in various scrapes, and in any case seems to have influenced nobody; the Mitchell group was not a jazz band but a ragtime band (although Bechet may have worked in it for a time); and the other groups, like Sam Wooding's, which made a long tour of the continent, were ordinary black show bands featuring a few jazz soloists. In fact, no important American group visited Europe between the Original Dixieland Jass Band's tour of 1919 and Armstrong's appearance in 1932. Popular interest was not there. There was no such thing, anywhere in Europe, as a cabaret which featured jazz full time,[8] and only a small number of real jazz records were issued until the end of the 1920s, and then only in a trickle. Although a few musicians were beginning to appreciate the music by the middle of the decade, on the basis of the few recordings available not more than a half-dozen Europeans could play it with any degree of skill before 1930.[9] The press ignored jazz almost totally. The London *Times* carried fourteen pieces on the music during the decade, mostly hostile, short, and uncomprehending. English magazines carried fewer than a dozen stories, also short, mainly hostile, and wholly concerned with symphonic jazz. There was no jazz—none at all—on radio. As late as 1927 the "Conductor of the Savoy Orpheans," probably either Debroy Summers or Carroll Gibbons (an American), wrote to the London *Times*, "The Savoy bands have been responsible for most of the dance music broadcast and listened to in Europe during the past four years" and added that they were not, in any case, jazz bands.[10] (One was a "Havana Band," the other a polite dance band.) Sid Colin, a British musician of the period, says in his book on British bands that the B.B.C. considered jazz to be "a nasty, noisy, alien nuisance, and they would have none of it."[11] Paul Specht reported in 1927 that "very little jazz music is heard by British radio listeners as a rule"[12]—which Specht, who was in the symphonic-jazz camp, thought was a good thing.

In the late 1920s a piano player named Fred Elizalde attempted to put together what probably can be called the first European jazz band, although the *jazz* in it was provided mainly by visiting Americans. Actually, the group was playing more a Whitemanesque version of the music, but even that was too noisy for British audiences and after two years it gave up.[13] Jim Godbolt says in his history of British jazz that in 1926 there were "no knowledgeable jazz buffs" in England.[14] Even in the early 1930s Max Jones, later to be a respected English jazz writer, said that England was "rather a jazz-starved land."[15]

The Gramophone, run for years by Compton McKenzie, began in 1923, and thus predated *Phonograph Monthly Review*. At first it offered a quarter of a column of reviews of dance music in every issue, but not until 1927 did it give even occasional mention to jazz, and only in 1930 did it begin to distinguish between jazz and ordinary dance music.

The *Melody Maker* was quicker to make the distinction. Founded at the beginning of 1926, it was similar to *Orchestra World*, although more comprehensive, better written, and eventually more successful. Like *Orchestra World*, it was concerned primarily with dance music and had relatively little to say about jazz. It did, however, run a few sporadic articles on jazz in its early issues. The first of these, which appeared in the magazine's second issue, was a piece describing jazz and giving a largely accurate, if brief, description of its origins in black New Orleans. The article was written by Bert Ralton, an American musician who had come to England with Art Hickman and had eventually settled there.[16] Ralton's piece was almost immediately forgotton: it would be another decade before British jazz writers understood the roots of jazz in early dixieland.

However, by 1927 the *Melody Maker*'s record reviewers were beginning to grasp the difference between good hot music and ordinary dance music. Their knowledge was sketchy and uneven, as it had to have been, working from such a distance. They generally favored the white dance bands, playing hot arrangements, to the black orchestras, which they saw as rhythmically interesting but otherwise crude and musically inferior. Morton's *The Chant* and *Black Bottom Stomp*, today considered masterpieces of the New Orleans genre, were "crude in orchestration and poor amusement to listen to"; the same review column gave high praise to Paul Whiteman's *Trudy*, now wholly forgotten.[17] In December 1928 a reviewer called another forgotten record, the Dorsey Brothers' *Was it a Dream?*, "without doubt the most wonderful and beautiful record ever made by a modern rhythmic combination."[18] Yet, as in America, the taste of the reviewers, especially a very young Patrick "Spike" Hughes, who was to become a force in the London jazz world, was gradually becoming firmer. Beiderbecke—who was referred to by the paper as "Bidlebeck" for some time—was quickly appreciated, and in 1927 the paper pointed out that Fletcher Henderson's "orchestrations are really excellent,"[19] although they had reservations about the band. Records by other important whites, like Eddie Lang, Joe Venuti, Miff Mole, Red Nichols, and Benny Goodman, were favorably reviewed, along with a great deal of quite poor stuff.

A good idea of the level of appreciation for jazz that had been reached in England toward the end of the 1920s can be had from a roundup of American bands written by Fred Elizalde and his brother Lizz, also a musician, in 1927.[20] The Elizalde brothers were sons of a Spanish diplomat; they were born in Manila and raised in the United States. They had been in the States as recently as the summer of the previous year, when they had recorded with a small group of their own, and they could probably claim to know as much about American jazz at that point as any European. They had high praise for a number of now-forgotten American dance-band musicians, if also for Benny Goodman and Jimmy Dorsey, who they said were unknown in England. They touted Armstrong, who was a "wonderful" trumpet player, and "Bidlebeck," who, they said, "is an amateur—at least he is a rich man and only plays for the fun of it. Like many artists, he's quite crazy in a mild way." It is clear that they had not heard Armstrong, and did not realize that he was black. They also had apparently not heard Beiderbecke, and they referred to Goodman as a saxophonist. They mentioned no blacks, aside from Armstrong.

Interest in jazz on the part of English intellectuals was almost entirely absent. In 1921 Clive Bell, who was at the center of the Bloomsbury group, England's most celebrated intellectual avant-garde circle, wrote,

> But jazz is dead, or dying at any rate . . . only the riff-raff has been affected. . . . The movement . . . was headed by a band and troupe of niggers, dancing. . . . Jazz art is soon created, soon liked, and soon forgotten. . . . Niggers can be admired artists without any gift more than high spirits.[21]

As late as 1928 Constant Lambert, who would eventually be cried up as one of the European intellectuals who discovered jazz, was writing,

> The point is that jazz has long ago lost the simple gaiety and sadness of the charming savages to whom it owes its birth, and is now, for the most part, a reflection of nerves, sex-repressions, inferiority complexes and general dreariness of the modern world. . . . Jazz, in fact, is just that sort of bastard product of art and life that provides so acceptable a drug to those incapable of really coping with either.[22]

Lambert was writing almost entirely about the symphonic jazz of Berlin and Gershwin, which in the United States was already losing favor to the hot bands; it is clear that he knew nothing about jazz as such at this time.

The French were even further behind, as they recognized. In a 1926 monograph called *Le jazz*, the authors say, "A l'heure actuelle, le jazz-band le plus complet est celui de Paul Whiteman"; and they added, "La diffusion du jazz est aujourd'hui si grande, en Amérique, que les ouvrages pédagogiques se sont multipliés. . . ."[23] Stephane Mougin, a pianist who was to become one of the first good French jazz musicians, wrote as late as 1931, "Hélas! Il n'y a pas en France de vrai jazz"; French musicians, he continued, were nothing but "de pales reflets de ces nouveaux romantiques d'Amérique."[24] In 1932 the *New York Times*'s Paris correspondent wrote that, until a short time before, "one could procure only with considerable difficulty some of Louis Armstrong's records. Those of Duke Ellington remained unknown. . . . All this has abruptly changed since the appearance of what we in Paris call 'le jazz hot'"[25]—a development triggered by Louis Armstrong's first European trip that summer. Charles Delaunay, one of the most important European jazz writers, has said that as late as about 1932 he thought he was the only jazz fan in France.[26] Hugues Panassié, even more influential than Delaunay, dated his own discovery of jazz to 1927, and only slowly developed his knowledge of it over the next years.[27] In 1927 the writer Irving Schwerké, who reported on music from Paris for several American publications, said,

> Jazz struck Europe a sharp blow. It fascinated hoi polloi and interested the intellectuals, but it must have been the magic of the name which charmed Europe, for so far as jazz *music* is concerned, very few Europeans have heard any, and ignorance of its true nature is general. . . . The ordinary American, it must be admitted, could not define jazz any better than the ordinary European, but where the American has the advantage is that his ear knows when it is jazz and when it is not.[28]

Schwerké is born out by the American jazz musician Bud Freeman, who went to Paris in 1928 and came back almost immediately: ". . . I found that the bands—the music would be bad, so I came back."[29]

Other countries of Europe were even farther behind. Robert Pernet, in a study of jazz in Belgium, reported that in the 1920s only eleven American bands, most of them now forgotten, visited that country, mainly for brief stays.[30] There was little other jazz activity. In Italy, "The first major milestone [in jazz] was the foundation of the jazz Hot Club in Milan in 1935," according to a writer on Italian jazz, Franco Fayenz.[31]

The first real European understanding of jazz began in the fall of 1929, when some editors from the *Melody Maker* visited New York expressly to study the music.[32] They discovered Duke Ellington running the house band at the Cotton Club, the country's best-known nightclub; Louis Armstrong and Fats Waller in *Hot Chocolates*, a hit show on Broadway, and doubling at Connie's Inn, second in renown only to the Cotton Club in Harlem; King Oliver at the fancy Quogue Inn on Long Island; and Fletcher Henderson at the Roseland Ballroom, the country's best-known dance hall. They were told about Earl Hines, working at an important new Chicago nightclub, the Grand Terrace. They became aware of the enormous output of good jazz on radio, the flood of jazz records coming into the shops every week. And they went home stunned, as their report in the *Melody Maker* makes clear. One of them wrote, "For every one place in London featuring dance or light popular music, there are about one hundred in New York."

At about the same time, Hugues Panassié in Paris was beginning to study the music. In 1927 he had heard some Red Nichols records and *Singing the Blues* and *I'm Coming, Virginia* of Bix and Tram.

Au bout de six mois, je commencera à sentir la supériorité de Bix sur les autres musiciens blancs. Louis Armstrong, Duke Ellington et les autres musiciens noirs m'étaient totalement inconnus à cette époque, à l'exception de l'orchestre Fletcher Henderson.[33]

His interest fired, Panassié began hearing a few Americans who were working with various dance bands around Paris, and gradually widened his understanding of jazz. Late in 1930 he began writing articles on jazz for *Jazz Tango*, which had just been founded. The magazine was essentially devoted to ordinary popular music, but Panassié used it as a vehicle for jazz pieces, publishing one in nearly every issue for several years. *Jazz Tango* also published occasional articles by others on jazz, especially Stephane Mougin; it also included some jazz record reviews along with its reviews of popular records.

Then, in 1934, Panassié published his celebrated book, *Le jazz hot*, with an English version following in 1936.[34] Its impact in Europe was substantial. Jazz fans there, who had little else to go on, fell upon it gratefully, and it quickly became their Bible. Even today, older European jazz fans feel a real debt to Panassié and resent attempts to point out his shortcomings.

Next, in March 1935, Panassié and some fellow members of the Hot Club of France founded *Jazz Hot*, which claimed to be the first magazine published anywhere that was devoted exclusively to jazz. It went on to become exceedingly influential, especially in Europe, although it was also read in the United States by a few students of the music.

Through the early thirties, then, comprehension of jazz in Europe increased rapidly among a small group of ardent enthusiasts. Louis Armstrong made visits in 1932 and 1933, Ellington in 1933, and first-hand exposure to these giants helped to educate European musicians, and to a lesser extent the European public, about jazz. After the Ellington trip, the *Melody Maker* said, "Ellington has been and thrilled thousands of us. So has Louis Armstrong. . . . Our education, woefully neglected, is being attended to. We now have everything to learn."[35] European jazz fans and musicians were eagerly buttonholing visiting American musicians, jazz writers like John Hammond (who came in 1933), and even ordinary tourists, and pelting them with questions about the music.

Yet, even though there was great enthusiasm for jazz among a small group of musicians and a handful of fans, the general European population was uninterested, and the audience for the music remained very small. Sid Colin, speaking of the early 1930s, said that, even then,

> Only a handful mastered [jazz] and immediately joined together in an elite; a group
> at once exalted and outcast, poet and pariah both, dedicating their lives to the mak-
> ing of music that only they and a tiny but devoted audience could comprehend and
> appreciate. As for making a living at it, there was simply no way.[36]

The Armstrong and Ellington appearances were triumphs as far as the musicians
were concerned, but did not attract wide audiences. In 1934, the *Melody Maker*
said, "It has been usual, during the London appearances of celebrated American
hot stars, for the fans to cheer themselves hoarse, but for the majority of the audience to register boredom, if not sheer dislike."[37] Neither Ellington nor Armstrong
were able to work regularly in Europe, even for brief periods; their appearances
were limited to occasional concerts or short runs as parts of variety bills. European
promoters recognized that they could sell these American jazz stars only as novelties
at widely spaced intervals. After 1933 no effort was made to bring either these two,
or any other important American jazz musicians, back to Europe until six years
later, when Ellington made a second tour.

The English critic Leonard Feather, writing for *Down Beat* from London in 1935,
said,

> To all you hopefuls who picture Europe as a haven of intelligence where everyone
> knows all about good jazz, let me begin by destroying your illusions right away. I
> was in New York for the first time last month, and came away with the impression
> that, however dumb your great U.S. public may be, ours is even dumber.[38]

Delaunay, who was at the center of European jazz activity, said, "Although isolated
jazz events had caused a great stir in Paris before the war—notably the Duke Ellington triumph of 1933—typical affairs of the Hot Clubs, even Paris sessions featuring
Django Reinhardt and Eddie South, drew only about 400 spectators."[39] And these
were not nightly events, but sporadic concerts.

In Europe, then, through the 1930s jazz remained the private hobby of a small clique.
There were no jazz clubs as such anywhere in Europe. In London, for example,
jazz was played at one or two after-hours clubs by a handful of musicians who loved
the music and who could come in and jam for drinks.[40] There was hardly any jazz
on the radio, and jazz records were issued in small editions, mainly by small labels
run almost as hobbies.

Jazz became popular in Europe only during the war. This was due in considerable
measure to the fact that Hitler had anathematized jazz as black and Jewish, and
therefore non-Aryan. Going to jazz concerts became, for the people of the captive

nations, a political act, and the audience for the music suddenly ballooned.[41] By the end of the war, traditional jazz had become the basic dance music for European students; even bebop was finding small audiences.

Since that time jazz has remained a presence in Europe. It has produced a steady stream of excellent jazz musicians; European record shops in many cities carry large stocks of jazz records, some of them offering better selections than many stores in the United States; jazz concerts and festivals are frequent and usually well attended; jazz periodicals, filled with the arcana of jazz scholarship, appear regularly. Europeans have produced many, many excellent studies of the music, particularly in the areas of jazz discography and musical analysis—both relatively easier to do at a distance than history or biography.

But, although jazz has had in the years after World War II a significant audience in Europe, it has never been a very large one. David Thomson, an American living in Paris, wrote in 1951,

> American critics have wasted a great deal of breath over the last 15 years lamenting the fact that Europeans, and especially the French, were the first to take our music seriously. . . . The bulk of Europe's jazz enthusiasts are still without any reasonable understanding of what the music is all about. The few experts may know their stuff, but the ordinary fan is nowhere.[42]

And in 1953 the New Orleans pioneer Zutty Singleton and his wife Marge, who had been told by Europeans that things were better there, fled Paris for the United States. Zutty told a *Down Beat* reporter:

> I saw [black American] musicians around there who'd been fooled by all the talk about how great things were, and now they were living from day to day, working for 2000 francs ($5) a night, just barely getting by. . . We actually feel freer in America than we did in France. . . . When I think of things like the night a fan told me he saw old Pops Foster trudging through the snow carrying his bass fiddle—because he couldn't afford a taxi—I wonder how people fall for all that stuff about conditions in Europe"[43].

On any statistical basis you wish to name—numbers of players, numbers of clubs, incomes of musicians, amounts of money spent on jazz records, books, live performances, or whatever else—American interest in the music has been far greater than European.

We should understand, moreover, that when we talk about the interest in jazz in "Europe" we really mean northwestern Europe, plus Switzerland and Italy.[44] There has never been any but the tiniest amount of jazz activity in Spain, Portugal, Greece, Turkey, or the Balkans. It is very difficult to hear any live jazz at all in Athens, Istanbul, Lisbon, or Barcelona—all cities with populations above two million—and impossible, aside from rare concerts, to hear any in smaller cities like Sevilla or Thessaloniki.

Similarly, there is not much live jazz played in eastern Europe. The picture here, of course, is complicated by politics: the attitude of the Soviet Union toward jazz has fluctuated between outright prohibition and reluctant acceptance, and in general the Eastern governments limit by a thicket of rules the amount of jazz that can be played. Yet even if we allow for political considerations, jazz interest in Rumania, Hungary, and similar places is small. For example, in few of the major cities is there any such thing as a regular jazz club, not even in Leningrad or Moscow. In Budapest, a couple of places offer jazz about once a week, for audiences that number a hundred or so people. Belgrade does not have a single jazz club. In Sofia there is no jazz at all, aside from occasional concerts and, in some periods, annual festivals. In Warsaw, which is considered the jazz capital of eastern Europe, there is a single club which offers jazz on a nightly basis as well as occasional jazz concerts. In the smaller cities jazz performances are rare, aside from student jam sessions.

Once again, there is a good deal more intellectual activity than is reflected in popular interest. *Jazz Forum*, a major international magazine, is published in Warsaw, and the International Jazz Federation, with which it is associated, is primarily a European institution. Jazz specialists in the Soviet Union circulate hundreds of privately translated jazz books, and there has even been official publication of good jazz books by outsiders, including Americans—in translations, however, that are not wholly reliable. The jazz audience in eastern Europe is intense but small.

The bulk of European jazz activity goes on in the capital cities of northwestern Europe—London, Paris, Amsterdam, Stockholm, Copenhagen—and in two or three cities in West Germany as well as Zurich, Rome, and Milan. These cities have had, over the past three decades or so, one to five jazz clubs each, at various times. However, this overstates the case. To a greater extent than is true in America, these clubs often feature part-time musicians who are paid nominal sums to play for crowds of students whose interest in jazz as such is quite variable. Outside of the capital cities, it is difficult to find full-time jazz clubs of any pretensions. There are presently some twenty true jazz clubs in New York, as opposed to three in London, four or five in Paris, one or two in Amsterdam. Moreover, virtually every American city of any size has at least one nightclub, and frequently more, offering jazz on a regular basis, in addition to concerts by visiting big names. Definitions of what constitutes a "true" jazz club are of course slippery; however, I estimate that there have been, in all of Europe, with a population roughly double that of the United States, on average over the past three decades thirty such clubs; in the United States, I estimate there have been a hundred.

It is true that in Europe a great deal of live jazz is played at concerts and festivals, of which there are some 200 annually,[45] rather than in clubs; although there are plenty of jazz concerts given in America, they are only a fraction of the number of jazz festivals that are put on annually in Europe. But attendance at many of these European festivals runs only to the hundreds, not the thousands; thus the total festival audience for jazz does not bulk all that large. Furthermore, most European festivals are subsidized by the governments, radio stations, record companies, and even sometimes, when American artists are involved, by the United States Department of State. Ticket prices are held unrealistically low. Some American jazz events, of course, are also supported by government grants or commercial sponsors, such as the companies that have aided the Newport Jazz Festival over the years. But in the main, jazz in the United States is supported by the public directly.

Nor is there in Europe anything like the immense jazz education system that exists in the United States, with hundreds of colleges and thousands of high schools—and even some junior high schools—offering jazz courses and training orchestras. The National Association of Jazz Educators has a membership of 6,000. Nor do European governments and private foundations offer the millions of dollars annually in grants, fellowships and scholarships that are available in the United States.

In sum, in Europe jazz has always played a secondary, if lively, role in the culture, somewhat akin to the interest in folk music in America; in the United States jazz has been, right from the beginning, a part of the cultural mainstream, known to all, understood to one degree or another by the majority, and of real interest to a substantial minority.

V

It is clear enough that the jazz audience in the United States has always been larger, and at times substantially larger, than the European one. Indeed, in the years before World War II the ratio was of the magnitude of one hundred to one. We have also seen that there was a substantial, if smaller, group of dedicated American jazz fans, numbering in the tens of thousands, and probable hundreds of thousands. As we have seen, *Time* magazine in 1937, when the swing boom was rising to a peak, estimated that there were a half-million "serious jazz fanciers" in the United States.[1] We have further seen that at least a few Americans, some of them important music critics, were writing seriously about jazz as early as 1917, when William Morrison Patterson made his analysis of jazz rhythm for the *Literary Digest*. This early critical writing was not made up of isolated pieces produced by a few lonely voices, but represented the visible portion of a widely held attitude among young intellectuals and music lovers that jazz was a peculiarly American invention which deserved informed attention.

The idea that jazz was discovered or "appreciated" first by Europeans, then, has to depend on something else. So the argument goes, Americans may well have gone out to dance and drink to jazz in larger numbers than Europeans, but it was Europeans who first saw it as a high art, and brought to it detailed analysis. As Eric Hobsbawm put it recently, jazz was so much a part of American life "that it was difficult for [Americans] to treat it as 'an art form,' and that it did not fit into American ideas about high culture in the early period."[2] On what, then, is this contention based?

The evidence customarily adduced to support the idea that Europeans were the first to write good jazz criticism in the early period is remarkably slim. The first document often referred to is a brief appreciation of Sidney Bechet by the Swiss conductor Ernest Ansermet, who heard Bechet with Will Marion Cook's Southern Syncopators in London in 1919. The piece has been widely reprinted in the jazz literature, usually in condensed form.[3] At the time, however, it attracted no attention, had no effect on the career of Bechet, who was apparently unaware of it, and was forgotten until a jazz researcher stumbled on it many years later. However prescient Ansermet may have been, American commentators like Walter J. Kingsley and William Patterson were making much more informed appraisals of the music two years earlier.[4]

There were a few early books on jazz published in Europe in the 1920s: André Coeuroy and André Schaeffner's *Le jazz*;[5] A. Baresel's *Das Jazz-Buch*;[6] and E. F. Burian's *Jazz*.[7] But these books were entirely concerned with the symphonic jazz of Whiteman, Gershwin, et al. and had nothing to say about the real thing. Similar books, like Whiteman's autobiography[8] and Henry O. Osgood's *So This Is Jazz*,[9] were being published in the United States at the same time.

European classical musicians were also taking an interest in jazz. Stravinsky, Debussy, and others were utilizing what they took to be ragtime and jazz in their music, for example the latter's *Golliwog's Cakewalk*. None of their works, however, showed a real comprehension of jazz. In fact, Americans themselves had been as quick to produce pseudo-jazz concert music: Charles Ives drew on ragtime as early as 1902,[10] John Alden Carpenter wrote a jazzy Concertino for piano and orchestra in 1915 and even subtitled his ballet score *Krazy Kat* (1921) a "jazz pantomine,"[11] and by 1925 Virgil Thomson was writing that "The taste of the moment in orchestra concerts would seem, from the pieces announced, to be largely for high-brow jazz. . . . A year ago every up-to-date composer in the land was engaged upon some sort of jazz piece."[12]

The first European who can make—and has made—the claim to have written serious jazz criticism is the Belgian Robert Goffin. In 1919 he published a piece in a literary journal called *Le disque vert* on the Louis Mitchell Jazz Kings; in 1920 he published a book of poems called *Jazz Band*, and in 1927 he took over a magazine called *Music*,[13] much of the content of which found its way into his book *Aux frontières du jazz* of 1932.[14] However, the Louis Mitchell group was not a jazz band but a ragtime dance orchestra made up of black U.S. Army bandsmen who had remained after World War I in Paris, where they had a modest temporary fame. A book of poems is not, of course, criticism, if we except Alexander Pope. That leaves us *Aux frontières du jazz*, which can fairly claim to be the first book to at least attempt to deal with what we today call the real jazz of the period.

Goffin's *Aux frontières du jazz* is a strange book, bearing a certain resemblance to a creature out of *Alice in Wonderland*. The first half of the book, more or less, consists of articles which apparently had been published elsewhere, many presumably in Goffin's magazine *Music*, among them his article on Mitchell's Jazz Kings. They exhibit an ignorance of the history and nature of jazz that is both wide and deep. According to Goffin's own story, in late 1924 he came across a California Ramblers' recording of *Southern Rose*, which contained a solo or break on saxophone by Jimmy Dorsey that was "possédé par une furie démoniaque." Excited, he played the record for Arthur Briggs, a black trumpeter who spent most of his adult life in Europe.

Briggs told him it was in the "New Orleans" manner of playing, and immediately Goffin went searching around record shops in Europe for more samples of the New Orleans style, apparently unaware that in the United States the music was no secret.[15] His education in jazz was thus extremely haphazard, and it is not surprising that his grasp of it for some time was poor. Furthermore, he had a tendency toward the romantic: for example, Irving Berlin, whom he considered an important jazz composer, "s'essaya à composer des airs où il sentait toute la malédiction des siens et la dévastation d'un monde religieux qu'il avait perdu"[16]—hardly a sensible thing to say about the composer of *Alexander's Ragtime Band* and *Marie from Sunny Italy*, two of Berlin's best-known early songs. Goffin knew nothing about the whole New Orleans period, and said he had searched in vain to discover "où, quand, comment le jazz est né,"[17] when it had long been accepted by Americans that it had originated in New Orleans. His article on the origins of jazz fails even to mention the Original Dixieland Jass Band, King Oliver, or any of the black New Orleans pioneers. He totally confused symphonic and hot jazz, called *Some of These Days* a "sublimé et extraordinaire" song created for the "superhuman" voices of Sophie Tucker, Louis Armstrong, and Cab Calloway.[18] His list of new stars who had recently appeared in the "firmament du jazz hot" includes some appropriate people like Jack Teagarden and Jimmy McPartland but also some who were never considered important jazz musicians, like Rube Bloom and Glenn Miller; it does not, however, include any blacks.[19] In general, the sections in the first half of *Aux frontiéres du jazz* concentrate on white groups, especially the California Ramblers, and white players like Red Nichols. (Beiderbecke is mentioned only once, in passing).

The remainder of Goffin's book is made up of short discussions of a whole raft of bands, and is much more knowledgeable than what went before. To be sure, Goffin gives a relatively large amount of space to the "jazz celebrities"—Paul Whiteman, Hal Kemp, and Ted Lewis—none of whom had been considered true jazz bands by informed Americans for years. But he does also offer reasonably correct, if thin, discussions of Armstrong, Ellington, Henderson, and many others.[20] It seems clear that this last section of *Aux frontières du jazz* was written expressly for the book, at a time when Goffin had begun to understand the music better than he had earlier. (It appears to me that he was quite dependent on Panassié and the *Melody Maker* for his information.) This latter material is not, certainly, on a level with the criticism being offered by Darrell and other Americans of the time, but it does reflect a growing understanding of jazz. What is difficult to grasp, therefore, is Goffin's failure to rewrite his earlier pieces—or abandon them altogether—when they are so frequently contradicted by material in the latter portion of the book. Readers must have found the book confusing, to say the least. Although it went through several printings very quickly in Europe, it was soon dismissed by the better-informed there, especially after the publication of Panassié's *Le jazz hot*. It was never translated into English.

In fact, by the time that Goffin's *Aux frontières du jazz* appeared, a number of other Europeans were better informed about jazz than he was. As we have seen (p. 44), the *Melody Maker* published a good, if brief, appraisal of jazz in 1926 by the American saxophonist Bert Ralton, but real understanding of the music only began in 1927. Over the next few years the people writing for the magazine came to comprehend the music better and better, especially after the fall 1929 trip of some of the editors to New York (see p. 46), but their understanding remained incomplete well into the 1930s: their judgments were sometimes on target, sometimes well off, both in aesthetic judgments and matters of fact. In 1932 Spike Hughes, generally believed to be the best British jazz critic of the time, called Ellington's *Creole Love Call* "the most insignificant and aimless record that Duke Ellington has ever produced,"[21] after calling *Creole Rhapsody* "the first classic of modern dance music" the previous year.[22] As we have seen, Darrell made just the opposite judgment about these two works, and it is his view that posterity has accepted. As late as 1934 Hughes remained unaware of the whole New Orleans tradition (as Europeans would through the decade), writing almost tentatively, "so there may well be a New Orleans style in jazz."[23]

Again, as late as 1934 the English Brunswick Record Company published a brochure on jazz which included a history of the music by Leonard Hibbs and a record round-up by Edgar Jackson, former publisher of the *Melody Maker*.[24] The history credited the Original Dixieland Jass Band with inventing jazz, failed to mention the seminal King Oliver and Jelly Roll Morton bands, and quoted Constant Lambert as saying that Louis Armstrong's music "quickly provokes a state of exasperation and ennui," because it is improvised rather than arranged.[25] The discussion of recordings in the brochure missed virtually all the significant ones, such as Ellington's *Black and Tan Fantasy*, Beiderbecke's *Singing the Blues*, and Armstrong's *West End Blues*. These were all major errors which no knowledgeable American would have made. Five years earlier Abbe Niles had picked Armstrong's *West End Blues* as one of the most important records of 1928,[26] and in 1932 Darrell wrote that in Armstrong ". . . hot jazz redeems a lively art from decay, foreshadows the more fluent, weightless music of the future. . . . Hearing Armstrong, one realizes that Lady Jazz is still articulate, still unregenerate and fecundly expressive."[27] Needless to say, it is the views of Niles and Darrell, not Lambert, that have prevailed.

A comparison of Darrell's and the *Melody Maker*'s treatment of Ellington's classic *Black and Tan Fantasy* may be worthwhile. Darrell singled the record out for special attention in the July 1927 issue of *Phonograph Monthly Review*, calling it "unusually interesting"; he subsequently reviewed two later versions by Ellington of the work, and discussed it again in his long essay on Ellington in *Disques* in 1932, where he said that when he first heard it, it had "a twisted beauty that grew on me more and more and could not be shaken off."[28] The *Melody Maker* writers, tipped off to the importance of the composition by Darrell's reviews, by chance acquired a version listed as by Louis Armstrong and his Original Washboard Beaters. (It was common at the time for versions of a tune to be issued by more than one company under different names). Spike Hughes reviewed it in the March 1928 issue, and it is clear from the context that neither he, nor presumably anybody else on the magazine, knew who either Armstrong or Ellington was.

Taken as a whole over the early years of the 1930s, the *Melody Maker* actually gave jazz very little attention. There was usually a fairly well-informed report from the United States by an American—John Hammond was the correspondent in February 1932—plus a page of increasingly sound reviews of hot jazz records being issued in England, but that was all, in a magazine that ran to over eighty pages.

A second British popular-music magazine, *Rhythm*, gave jazz even less attention. During 1931 it ran a series of brief commentaries on popular music by American musicians, but these were almost totally concerned with dance music. Beginning in 1932 the magazine reviewed dance records, and included some good jazz discs among them. But that was all the attention the magazine paid to jazz. *Orkester Journalen*, a dance-band magazine published in Stockholm, founded in 1933, gave jazz no coverage whatever until 1935, when it began running reports on dance music from the United States which occasionally touched upon good jazz. Another magazine, *Revue du jazz*, carrying articles by Stephane Mougin, Phillippe Brun, and other French jazz musicians, had a brief life in 1929. It was essentially covering dance music, and showed little comprehension of the difference between symphonic jazz and the hot version. It is said to have had "little influence, since almost the only people who read it were those who also wrote for it."[29] Finally, in 1935 there appeared in England a short-lived but very good jazz magazine called *Hot News*, which lasted for six issues. It was certainly the best jazz periodical published to that date, but its career was too brief for it to have much effect.[30]

This brings us to the figure of Hugues Panassié, who dominated European jazz criticism until after World War II, when he began to feud with the supporters of bebop and rapidly lost his influence. In fact, the case for the priority of European appreciation of jazz rests to a substantial extent on Panassié's shoulders. He was not the only European writing about jazz in the 1930s, of course: there were Goffin, Hughes, the Dutch author Joost Van Praag, and a few others. But Panassié alone was regularly writing serious critical articles about jazz, and there was, of course, his book *Le jazz hot.* If we subtract the substantial body of writing by Panassié from the whole, we are not left with very much: some record reviews in the *Melody Maker, Rhythm,* and a few other magazines; a handful of pieces by Mougin, Van Praag, and others; and Goffin's maladroit *Aux frontières du jazz.* How, then, does Panassié's work compare with that of the Americans? Did he truly show them the way?

In 1930 Panassié began publishing regular monthly articles in *Jazz Tango.* There were pieces on Armstrong, Ellington, Teagarden, other jazz trombonists, and the like. They were generally a page or two in length, and, as was the case with Hughes in the *Melody Maker,* Panassié's arrows sometimes hit the target, sometimes landed out in the woods. He said of Armstrong, "Un Bix y a puisé la moitié de son inspiration. Un Muggsy [Spanier] est parvenu à coïncider complètement."[31] In fact, Armstrong, Beiderbecke, and Spanier played in three very different styles: Beiderbecke built his style on that of Nick LaRocca before he had ever heard Armstrong, and Spanier's main model was King Oliver, a mute specialist, although it is true that for a brief period he attempted to model himself on Armstrong. The list of Armstrong recordings accompanying the article included Ellington's *Black and Tan Fantasy*—the one which had also confused Spike Hughes. Either Panassié had never actually heard the record, or, like Hughes earlier, he could not tell Armstrong from Bubber Miley, Ellington's trumpeter.

In 1931 Panassié wrote of Spanier,

> On peut même avancer qu'il est, depuis la madadie [*sic*] de Bix, le cornet le plus près de Louis Armstrong. . . . Tous les efforts de Muggsy tendent à copier Louis Armstrong note par note. . . . Ainsi Louis Armstrong à ses débuts imitant King Oliver.[32]

Now, although all jazz musicians of the day were influenced by Armstrong, Spanier, as I have said, became a mute specialist in imitation of Oliver, and Armstrong, to the contrary, was not influenced by Oliver. The latter played in a small physical and emotional compass; Armstrong was a bravura and strongly emotional player who flew around the horn and rarely used mutes (and then usually a simple straight mute). One must remember that when Armstrong was serving his apprenticeship in New Orleans after 1917, Oliver was in Chicago and on the West Coast; Armstrong did not hear Oliver play during this early formative period. Panassié's errors were not minor ones; the subject was lines of influence among seminal figures, and his mistakes suggest that he either was incapable of making good musical judgments or had never heard any of Oliver's recordings, which I think was probably the case.

Again, in 1931, under the title "Les grands trombones hot" Panassié made that mixture of sound comment and poor judgment that would always be typical of his writing. In a previous issue he had written at length about the glories of Jack Teagarden.[33] Now he announced that Jimmy Harrison and Dicky Wells were the leading black trombonists, but then went on to say: "Très près de ces deux trombones noirs, nous pouvons placer Tommy Dorsey qui est le meilleur après Jack Teagarden, si l'on considère seulement l'élément blanc."[34] Panassié was right about Harrison and Wells, wrong about Dorsey, as even Dorsey would have said. He went on to say that Dorsey had begun to play like Teagarden, which was certainly not true. He then added to his list of "grands trombones hot" Herb Flemming, Albert Wynn, and "Cuffee Davidson," and concluded that for another great trombonist one had to turn to a Frenchman, Léon Vauchant. The neglected Wynn was a very good trombonist, but Flemming was not, nor was he, as Panassié claimed, a follower of Teagarden. "Cuffy Davidson" was presumably Ed Cuffee, a journeyman trombonist with McKinney's Cotton Pickers; and Leo Vauchant, as he is generally called, does not belong on anyone's list of great trombonists. At the time, Panassié was apparently unaware of such excellent trombonists as Kid Ory, who had recorded with Oliver and on the important Armstrong Hot Fives; Charlie Green, the premier trombonist with Henderson in the 1920s; and J. C. Higginbotham, then with the Luis Russell orchestra.

Later in the same year, in an article about Bix Beiderbecke, Panassié said,

> Alors que tous les musiciens hot blanc détestaient la façon de jouer des nègres et méprisaient ceux qui l'appréciaient, Bix eut le courage—et non pas seulement le courage de la volonté mais aussi celui du jugement—de s'arracher à ce préjugé et d'aller avec son ami Muggsy—autre grand pionnier du style hot—dans les cabarets de Chicago écouter Louis Armstrong, de s'en imprégner de se mettre à jouer dans sa manière.[35]

Panassié almost certainly got this idea from Spanier, whom he knew in Paris for a period. But as we have seen, although Spanier and Beiderbecke certainly went into the Chicago black-and-tans to hear Armstrong, neither formed his style on Louis's. Furthermore, while it is true that some American dance-band musicians detested the "nigger style," a great many were drawn to it. Virtually every important jazz musician of the period visited, and frequently, the places where blacks played. As early as 1922 the management of Lincoln Gardens was putting on those midnight rambles specifically for white musicians. A little later, as Earl Hines remembered, Benny Goodman, Bix Beiderbecke, Hoagy Carmichael, the Dorsey brothers, Joe Sullivan, Jess Stacy, and other whites were coming to listen at the Sunset Cafe, where Hines was playing with Armstrong, or the Plantation, where

Oliver was playing.[36] In 1929, when Armstrong came to New York to play a brief engagement, a group of white musicians held a banquet for him and presented him with a watch engraved "To Louis Armstrong, the World's Greatest Cornetist, from the Musicians of New York."[37] In 1930 *Variety* reported that he was "the model of innumerable collegiate orchestras."[38] In the same year the American correspondent for the *Melody Maker* said that Armstrong was at a Harlem night club and that "musicians, of course, flock up to hear him."[39] Once again, Panassié's remark about Bix was not a minor error, for it suggested that the influence of blacks on whites, who "detested" them, was negligible.

As a consequence of the *Jazz Tango* pieces, by the early 1930s Panassié was coming to see himself as an authority on what was to Europeans a new music, and he set about writing his book *Le jazz hot*. The work went on to become the Bible of jazz for Europeans, who at this point had nothing else to go on and fell upon it eagerly. Unfortunately, it was chaotic and badly informed; once again, sound insights were mixed with fantasy, legend, and in some cases pure invention. It would be pointless to detail all of the errors in the book; I will discuss only a few of the obvious ones. For example, Panassié's account of the origin of early black music is wholly phantasmagorical: Some blacks were driving huge stones into the earth to bulwark a levee, and to make the work easier they executed it in rhythm; "Their lamentations became rhythmic songs . . . years later the black slave, now become a free citizen, would teach his children as he strummed an old banjo these sad songs of his ancestors: St. Louis Blues, Memphis Blues, New Orleans Blues."[40] The work song, of course, had a tradition reaching back to Africa; moreover, the songs specifically cited were commercial tunes written for Tin Pan Alley. Panassié also manufactured a naive aesthetic depending on "intonations," "rhythmic intervals," and "vibratos" which had nothing to do with the way the musicians themselves thought about the music. He apparently had never heard, or heard of, the seminal Creole Jazz Band recordings and entirely missed the importance of the band. Similarly, he failed to grasp the enormous impact that the Original Dixieland Jass Band discs had not only on jazz but American popular music in general. He said that the hot style appeared in 1926,[41] thus being oblivious to the whole New Orleans tradition, which was thirty years old at the time he was writing.

The book is rife with smaller errors as well. Panassié says of Armstrong: "Often he would be quite motionless as he played or sang . . . tears would roll down his cheeks."[42] He could hardly have heard Armstrong perform, for Louis was in constant motion as he played, and mugging and grinning, as early films show. Panassié says that Beiderbecke introduced the cornet to jazz while "the Negroes stuck to the trumpet,"[43] whereas not a single one of the early New Orleans blacks used the trumpet, and only switched to it in the mid-1920s on Armstrong's example. He says again that Bix was influenced by Joe Smith and Armstrong,[44] whereas Beiderbecke had formed his style on that of Nick LaRocca. He says that the Armstrong style suddenly appeared in 1919 or 1920,[45] when in fact Armstrong was still an unknown musician in New Orleans in those years, and had never recorded.

Hot Jazz, as the English language version was called, was never taken very seriously by knowledgeable people in the United States. Otis Ferguson said in 1939 that it was

> . . . somewhat exhausting, because of its mixture of disorganization, rapture and inevitable remoteness from the tradition and general work of the case in point. . . . His book is still available and a standard source of extremely valuable misinformation.[46]

E. Simms Campbell, in the competing *Jazzmen*, said,

> Not that M. Panassié is insincere, neither are "jitterbugs" insincere—but an intellectual approach to the blues that borders on the ridiculous with the attendant erudite mumbo-jumbo is doing one of the purest forms of American music much more harm than good.[47]

Sidney Finkelstein in his 1948 book said, "Today its theories no longer stand up."[48] Franklin Marshall Davis, who wrote about jazz for the black press, said, "The Panassié book was looked upon as an oddity by the few blacks who heard of it."[49]

The book has stuck in the craw of American jazz writers ever since it was published. They were angry at themselves for having let this Frenchman steal a march on them, especially as many of them felt that they could have written a far better book. Several of them set out to do so, resulting in the publications in 1938 and 1939 of Ramsey and Smith's *Jazzmen*, Sargeant's *Jazz: Hot and Hybrid*, and Hobson's *American Jazz Music*[51]—all substantially better than the Panassié volume. Their attitude was expressed years later by Hammond, who still felt called upon to insist, "I was in this long before Panassié was, and I knew musicians and he didn't know any musicians."[52]

Whatever the Americans thought, Panassié's book established his reputation as a major authority on jazz—*the* authority, in the view of many Europeans—and it led directly to the founding of the magazine *Jazz Hot* in 1935. This was, on the whole, a pretty good jazz magazine, especially considering the fact that it was being published at a distance from the subject. However, it is difficult to see how the magazine could have been successful without American help. About a third of the major articles were written by Americans, including John Hammond, Marshall Stearns, Preston Jackson, George Frazier, Helen Oakley, and Wilder Hobson, some of the best American critics of the time. Moreover, the European contributors were reading whatever American writing they could find on the subject. Goffin, for example, had somehow got hold of some of the early *Literary Digest* articles while working on his book; the *Melody Maker* people were following Darrell; and Panassié, if he were not reading Darrell directly, was seeing the *Melody Maker*. They were also reading *Down Beat* after it began in 1934.[53] And of course they were all falling on the few American jazz musicians who visited Europe from time to time, to dig information out of them. According to Charles Delaunay, Freddy Johnson, a black piano player who spent a lot of time in Europe, was particularly important:

> . . . he taught us how to tell the difference on Fletcher Henderson records between the trumpet players Joe Smith and Tommy Ladnier and Rex Stewart. It was difficult to identify soloists before that. We learned the history of jazz through his words.[54]

Benny Carter, who lived in England and France during much of the 1930s, was also important.[55] There was also Arthur Briggs, who was consulted by Goffin and others from time to time. It is thus fair to say that *Jazz Hot* magazine was a collaboration, with the Americans making a substantial and essential contribution.

Given the muddled nature of the Europeans' jazz education, dependent as it was on sources which themselves were not always reliable, it is hardly surprising that, however enthusiastic and serious, their writing was frequently factually incorrect and filled with judgments that have not held up. The problem with Panassié in particular was his willingness to rush into print long before he was properly prepared to do so. Furthermore, it seems to me that when first-hand information was lacking, he would offer his readers whatever anybody had told him. For example, I do not believe that he had heard Oliver when he first began writing about him. He cannot have heard more than one or two brief Dicky Wells solos in 1931, when he placed him atop the trombone pantheon, since Wells had hardly recorded at that time. Similarly, he was writing with enthusiasm about Art Tatum when Tatum had not made more than a couple of records,[56] and those in a style quite different from the one he would become famous for. It is my suspicion that in cases like these Panassié was told by someone that an Oliver, a Wells, a Tatum, was a brilliant new find and he simply put the information in print.

Furthermore, Panassié had, as Europeans frequently have, a tendency to over-rate players he had heard in person, like Léon Vauchant and Herb Flemming. Worse, it is my feeling that he allowed his enthusiasm to sweep him across the line into fantasy occasionally. I find it hard to believe that someone told him that Armstrong stood motionless when he played, with tears running down his face, unless that someone was simply pulling his leg; my hunch is that here Panassié allowed his romantic impulses to run away with him.

Working at so great a distance from the source, Panassié could not have been expected to get it all right. Indeed, it is remarkable that he got as much right as he did. But he made one serious mistake: not to visit the United States himself. Two or three months in New York and Chicago in 1930 would have allowed him to write a good book about jazz, and might truly have entitled him to claim to be the first jazz critic. But he did not come. Like other Europeans, he appeared to view the United States as an anthropologist views an indigenous tribe in the South African bush or the Australian outback: you had, of course, to dig information out of the natives; but you would hardly ask them to interpret your findings. However, anthropologists usually go to the outback to see the tribe in its environment. This Panassié did not do, and the consequence was that he was not able, in these early years, to write about jazz as knowledgeably as the Americans like Darrell and Hammond could.

One more European writer who has often been pointed to as an example of earlier appreciation of jazz abroad than at home is Constant Lambert. Lambert was a composer who has been termed "the architect of English ballet music."[58] He had an obsession with blacks and Asiatics, and was inevitably drawn to the occasional black shows which visited London.[59] He was first excited by "jazz" in 1922, when he saw an American show called *Dover Street to Dixie*, which featured singer Florence Mills and Will Vodery's Plantation Orchestra.[60] Over the 1920s, he saw two or three more similar shows, and he concluded that the music in them was jazz. It was not, and Lambert really never understood the music at all, as is clear from the 1928 piece by him quoted earlier (see p. 45).

It is very much to the point—as I shall discuss in more detail later—that at this moment, in the early 1930s, nobody, Europeans or Americans, believed that the former were introducing the latter to the virtues of jazz. The Europeans were heavily dependent on Americans for both information and critical insight. John Hammond and Rob Darrell were particularly influential—Hammond because he visited Europe from time to time and was writing for *The Gramophone* and the *Melody Maker*, Darrell because of his *Phonograph Monthly Review* and *Disques* pieces. Darrell's influence on the English, and through them the French, has never been acknowledged. His reviews and general articles were known in England: Hibbs referred to him as "a well-known American authority," and a letter to *Disques* signed "Parlophone Co. Ltd" said, "We read *Disques* every month."[61] In 1932 Edgar Jackson, formerly of the *Melody Maker*, wrote Darrell asking permission to reprint Darrell's Ellington piece in the Brunswick Records brochure. He added that he had read Darrell's work "with the deepest interest and admiration" and (ironically, in the context of the present discussion) requested permission to make changes in Darrell's writing since the article was "obviously written for a more intellectual public than it will reach here, and some of the words used in the opening chapter may be beyond their understanding."[62] One of the pieces of evidence for priority of European appreciation of jazz has been the fact that analyses of Ellington's work by Constant Lambert in 1933, during Duke's first trip to Europe, awoke in Ellington the sense that he was a real composer and ought to take his music seriously.[63] And it is certainly true that the encouragement of Lambert, Hughes, and others convinced Ellington to write those "Negro Rhapsodies and tone poems" that Darrell hoped he would stay away from. But Darrell had been an avid supporter of Ellington before the English knew anything about him, and his writing on Ellington was better than the Europeans. It is hard to believe that the English were uninfluenced by Darrell's articles.

In sum, Panassié and the other Europeans were, in the early 1930s, writing serious jazz criticism but it was not very good criticism, as it hardly could be, considering that they had only begun to hear the music—Panassié had only known about it for three years when he began writing on it for *Jazz Tango*—and were a long way from the source. To Americans jazz was a live music, which they heard in clubs and dance halls; to Europeans it was solely a recorded music, and what they heard was only a distored reflection of what Americans were seeing and hearing at home.

What, meanwhile, were the Americans doing by way of jazz writing? Ironically, the very years in which Europeans were beginning to write about jazz were precisely the years in which Americans stopped writing about it. In 1929 the stock market collapsed, and the country rapidly sank into a horrendous financial crisis which would change forever the character of American society. The effects of the Depression on jazz were substantial. It badly hurt the nightclubs, which had always been dependent on the big spender out on the town. The record industry, faced with competition from radio, which was free, came close to dying: sales which in the 1920s had run above 100 million copies a year, dropped to 6 million.[64] People found they could dance at home to radio, or to the records they already owned, and the dance halls suffered. At the same moment, the arrival of talking pictures threw out of work thousands of musicians who had been playing for silent films. The net result was that a lot of jazz musicians found themselves struggling, or even out of work.[65] In the early 1930s Sidney Bechet, for example, was running a tailor shop.[66]

Jazz writing suffered accordingly. To many people, it seemed that the music had been a fad, like ragtime, whose day had passed. Media interest in it decreased: between 1930 and 1935 major American magazines ran only eighteen pieces on jazz, or about one-third the number they had been running. *Phonograph Monthly Review* and *Disques* folded. *Orchestra World*, which in the 1920s had given jazz bands at least some attention, stopped covering jazz at all.

However, despite this decline in overt jazz activity, there is no evidence that American interest in the music had fallen off. There continued to be a steady amount of jazz played on the radio. Some of the dance halls and cabarets survived; the Cotton Club and other Harlem clubs remained profitable for some years.[67] And of course people went on playing the records they had bought when times were good. Indeed, despite the collapse of the record industry, the surviving companies issued some 1,000 jazz sides during this period, among them many records today considered classics.[68] The Ellington, Armstrong, and Casa Loma orchestras worked continuously through the period—ironically, the only times Armstrong did not work full-time were during his European visits of 1932 and 1933–34.[69]

Then, with the enormous success of the Benny Goodman band in 1935 and the swing-band boom which followed, it became clear that jazz had never been dead in the United States, only held down by the effects of the financial cataclysm. American jazz criticism instantly revived; or, to put it perhaps more accurately, it came up into daylight again, for obviously a lot of jazz fans had continued to study the music all along. Marshall Stearns had been "trying to read all the writings on jazz, listen to all the recordings of jazz, and talk to all the musicians who play jazz" he could discover since the late 1920s;[70] by 1932 Rudi Blesh was interviewing older musicians towards a book on jazz;[71] in the same year Darrell interviewed Armstrong and Ellington, and was trying to get Ellington to cooperate in a biography (see p. 40). John Hammond, who had been writing on jazz for the *Melody Maker* and concentrating on social issues in the United States—he covered the Scottsboro Boys trial for *The Nation*—turned in 1935 to writing about jazz for the American press.[72]

In particular, *Down Beat*, founded as a dance-band magazine focused on Chicago, where it was published, rapidly became in essence a jazz magazine, although it continued to cover dance-band musicians, trade controversies, and a good deal of claptrap. By 1935 it was running pieces by Hammond, Stearns, Helen Oakley, George Frazier, and others—the very people who were doing so much writing for *Jazz Hot*. By the end of 1935, when both magazines had been in existence for about a year, *Down Beat* was as good a jazz magazine as *Jazz Hot*, running the same sort of serious pieces mixed in with the claptrap but as a rule inevitably more accurate.

But *Down Beat* was not alone in carrying material on jazz. The *American Music Lover*, begun in May 1935 as a classical-music periodical, carried excellent reviews by "Van"—Horace Van Norman—of what it called "hot jazz" from its first issue.

For example, in a review of Goodman's *King Porter Stomp* and *Sometimes I'm Happy*, "Van" said, in part,

> These are both elegant arrangements by Fletcher Henderson and reveal Goodman's great band at its very best. Bunny Berigan celebrates his entrance into the band by doing some of the same sort of work which has helped to put him on the very top shelf of trumpet players.[73]

Berigan's solo on *Sometimes I'm Happy* is one of his best.

In February 1936 *American Music Lover* added a column called "Swing Music Notes" by Enzo Archetti, who also began writing for it occasional full-dress articles on jazz. Also in 1936, Otis Ferguson began contributing regular articles on jazz to the *New Republic*, quickly developing a reputation as possibly the country's best jazz writer of the day, and good jazz articles appeared in *American Mercury, Harper's, Scholastic, Scribner's*, and the *Literary Digest*.[74] The *Harper's* piece, significantly subtitled "Rediscovering Jazz," was especially good—erudite and intelligent—and said, among other things, "Simple in its essence, jazz has now become an intensely complex, highly developed art." And in 1938 the first of the American "little" magazines on jazz, the *H.R.S. Society Rag*, came into being.[75]

All of this activity finally led, over the next decade or so, to a spate of books on jazz, all of them substantially better than Panassié's or Goffin's: in addition to Sargeant's *Jazz: Hot and Hybrid* (1938), Ramsey and Smith's *Jazzmen* (1939), and Hobson's *American Jazz Music* (1939), cited above (see p. 60), there were Rudi Blesh's *Shining Trumpets* (1946), Sidney Finkelstein's *Jazz: A People's Music* (1948), and finally Marshall Stearns's *The Story of Jazz* (1956), the best book on the subject to that point and still a useful, although somewhat dated, introduction to the subject. But jazz, after 1935, was not being written about in the United States solely for a small, specialized audience, as it was in Europe. Popular magazines like *Esquire* and intellectual magazines like the *New Republic* were running frequent articles on jazz; and by the late 1930s the great national magazines such as *Life* and the *Saturday Evening Post* were printing occasional jazz features, some of them quite good. This work, much of it produced by people who had been studying the music before the Europeans knew about it, was from any point of view sounder than what Panassié and company, with the best will in the world, could be expected to do.

It should not be thought that this sudden revival of interest in jazz was triggered by the writings of the Europeans. *Jazz Tango* was hardly known in the United States—I have seen no reference to it in any American writing of the period—and in any case was in French, a language not necessarily read by jazz fans and musi-

66

cians. Goffin's book was known to some people, but it too was in French, and because of its idiosyncrasies had little influence even among those who had read it. Panassié's book was published in English only in 1936; although a few Americans read it in French, that was not until 1935, when the American revival was already underway. Similar, Panassié's magazine *Jazz Hot* did not start up until 1935, so could not have had much effect on the jazz boom here. Actually, the reason for the sudden efflorescence of writing on jazz was quite simple: because of the swing boom, jazz had once again become a broad cultural phenomenon, and magazines both popular and highbrow were willing to run reports on it.

But it is nonetheless true that for a few years—let us say from 1932, when Darrell left *Phonograph Monthly Review*, to 1935, when *Down Beat* started to run a good deal of jazz commentary—the Europeans were publishing more jazz criticism than the Americans were. Thus, at the beginning of 1935, if you had been unaware of the writings on jazz in America in the 1920s, and compared recent American and European jazz writing, you could easily have concluded that Europeans were the first to appreciate jazz. That was precisely the position of the Europeans: except for Darrell's work in *Disques* and *Phonograph Monthly Review*, they had read little of the American writing of the 1920s—little American jazz writing of any kind. Even today, it is doubtful of *any* European jazz authority has heard of Darrell, Ferguson, or Niles; and they know of Van Vechten only as the author of *Nigger Heaven*. Thus, when the Europeans looked around in 1935 they saw at home the Panassié and Goffin books, Panassié's articles in *Jazz Tango*, the brand new magazine *Jazz Hot* proclaiming itself to be the first ever jazz magazine, and reviews of jazz records in the *Melody Maker*, *Rhythm*, and other periodicals. They saw nothing comparable in the United States.

But the Americans knew better—or should have. Yet even as the revived interest in jazz was making the music a national phenomenon once again, the idea was taking hold that Europeans had been the first to discover jazz as a serious music, and were leading the way for the Americans in appraising it.

VI

How is it possible that virtually every serious student of jazz, both at home and abroad, believes that Americans hated the music and left its discovery to Europeans? How could such a myth sustain itself in the face of facts which are thoroughly documented, obvious, and known to a great many people, including some who were actually active in sustaining the myth? It has been, as we shall see, a fascinating case of mass self-deception, of a whole group of people managing to believe what they wanted to believe, despite the facts.

The creation of this myth about the reception of jazz began with a misperception on the part of jazz musicians and entertainment people in general, especially black ones. By the 1920s the word was out among black entertainers that things were better in Europe. In 1921 a black singer, Frank Dennie, wrote from London to the Chicago Defender, a black newspaper, that

> . . . thank the Lord, you don't run into the "color line" every time you turn around. . . . There are so many of our boys over here now that on a warm afternoon as one passes the corner of High and Denmark Streets [the musicians' area] . . . he almost imagines that he is at 35th and State Streets.[1]

The word was not entirely correct; there was plenty of race prejudice in Europe, as there still is: Louis Armstrong had to try a dozen hotels in London in 1932 before he could find one that would take him;[2] the next year Duke Ellington's men had considerable difficulty finding accommodations, and went home somewhat disillusioned.[3] Nonetheless, things were better for blacks in Europe—after all, Europeans were exploiting non-whites in Africa and Asia, whereas Americans were doing it at home. Blacks could not get into all the hotels or restaurants in Europe, but they could get into some; by contrast, until after World War II it was impossible for a black, except for a tiny handful of public figures, to get into any white hotel in America.

When Armstrong and the Ellington group came to England they not only found themselves able to meet whites on a social basis more easily than at home but were surrounded by avid groups of fans, among them titled gentlemen, eager to talk to them about their work. Not surprisingly, they failed to see beyond the small circle of admirers to a general public that was indifferent to jazz or actually hostile to it.

As I have noted (p. 2), the European writers Timme Rosenkrantz and Ian Carr have pointed to the uproars that occurred when Louis Armstrong appeared in Copenhagen and Charlie Parker in Paris as examples of Europe's greater appreciation of these musicians. The musicians inevitably saw it that way, too. But they all missed the point: Armstrong and Parker were cried up abroad because the presence there of an important jazz musician, at that time, was a rarity. In America such men were commonplaces, part of the regular scenery, and were coming and going constantly. They would have found it annoying to be regularly met at trains by hordes of ecstatic fans prepared to carry them away on their shoulders. American musicians resident in Europe have noticed the effect: celebrated at first, they discover the interest in them drops quickly once they become "locals."

American jazz musicians even today are prone to the same misperception. The American star on a two-week tour of Europe flies into some place like Lisbon or the North Sea Jazz Festival in Holland, tired from travel, to be met by greeting committees, reporters, and eager fans; he is given a tumultuous ovation when he appears on stage; and he is dragged off to jam with local musicians after the concert (when he would far rather go to bed). The next morning he leaves on a flood of good will. When this pattern is repeated a dozen times in fourteen days, he can hardly be blamed for going home thinking that his music is better loved abroad than at home.

What he fails to perceive, of course, is that after his departure, when the concert is done or the festival over, local jazz activity dwindles to a small trickle or dries up altogether. A jazz concert, especially one featuring American stars, is a significant event in a place like Lisbon, Athens, even Amsterdam or Copenhagen. It will attract not only all the serious jazz fans from a considerable distance but also a great many people whose interest in jazz is modest but who want to be in on the event—just as, for example, in America a lot of people who rarely attend the ballet will turn out for a performance by a Russian company.

Furthermore, jazz has always been seen by many Europeans, especially students, as anti-establishment. In western Europe it continues, for political reasons, to attract a lot of young people on the left. Paradoxically, in eastern Europe, for precisely the same reason, it is seen as "freedom music," and attracts the antis.

The jazz audience which so impresses the visiting American musician is thus to a degree exaggerated by both social and political concerns; but he takes the momentary bubble of jazz activity as the norm. This misperception is twisted further by the difficulty that many American jazz musicians, especially young ones, have in getting jobs playing jazz in New York, Chicago, and elsewhere. Their natural tendency is to blame it all on the public: if they are not working, it must be because the American people do not like jazz. What they fail to understand is that with colleges turning out literally thousands of trained jazz musicians every year, many of them excellent, it would be impossible for any social system, no matter how avid its interest in jazz, to absorb more than a fraction of them—as indeed the American system cannot possibly absorb all the thousands of graduates of journalism schools, dance studios, or art institutes. A strange phenomenon of the American middle class today is that it is training a huge proportion of its young people for careers that do not exist, and leaving them as unemployable as the ghetto high school drop-out. Thus, the young jazz musician without a gig sees the glass as half empty, when compared with the European situation it is actually half full.

The musicians, then, were the first to believe that things were "better in Europe," and it did not take much effort for them to convince European jazz writers that this was the case. Unfortunately, the writers did not come to the States to see for themselves. It is surprising how many European jazz critics have not made the effort to visit the United States. Hugues Panassié wrote a whole book on jazz without coming to America, which is a little like an American writing a book on French cooking without visiting France. The same is true of Goffin; and Charles Delaunay had written about jazz for fifteen years, establishing himself as one of the world's foremost authorities on the subject, before he set foot in the United States. To be sure, by the mid- to late 1930s some Europeans, like Timme Rosenkrantz, were making regular visits; and others extended visits into full-time American careers, among them the English writers Leonard Feather and Stanley Dance. But many others did not come, or visited only occasionally and briefly. These Europeans, then, could believe that the visiting American musicians were right when they said that jazz was better appreciated in Europe than in the United States: they had no basis for judging the truth.

The groundwork for the building of the myth that jazz was despised at home and had to be discovered by Europeans was thus laid first by the misperceptions of jazz musicians themselves, and second by the willingness of Europeans to accept what the musicians were telling them. The myth could not have come into being, however, had it faced a concerted attack by Americans. What it got was just the reverse: for through the late 1930s, and into the 1940s, a growing number of American jazz writers, in the burgeoning little jazz magazines and in the books which had begun to appear, were saying the same thing—that jazz was, and always had been, a ghetto music despised by the middle class, and appreciated only by a small minority of perceptive whites and Europeans. How could this have happened?

The idea that America was a cultural wasteland which had to look to Europe for art, literature, and philosophy has a long history. Through the eighteenth and nineteenth centuries it was taken for granted in both Europe and the United States that the Europeans led in these fields, and Americans who were wealthy enough made extended visits to Europe in order to gain cultivation.[4]

By the twentieth century, however, a good many American intellectuals were beginning to say that the United States was now the fresh new voice and that Americans no longer had to look east for their arts and letters, as Malcolm Cowley makes clear in his classic *Exile's Return*;[5] R. D. Darrell's insistence on the worth of American music was typical of this viewpoint.

But the older view lingered. Particularly important in promoting the idea that Americans were material-minded philistines, lacking the artistic sensibility of the Europeans, was H. L. Mencken, one of the most influential social critics of the 1920s. "The country is irrevocably rotten," Mencken wrote Theodore Dreiser, and in another letter he added, "I am more and more convinced we had better reach out for European audiences. The United States will go from bad to worse."[6] Mencken was read by exactly the young artists and intellectuals who were in the jazz camp, and he helped to keep alive the idea that America was a cultural sink.

Thus, the idea that jazz was first appreciated by the Europeans would have fit into the preconceptions of many of these early jazz writers. Who first proposed it is hard to say, but it appears in print first—so far as I have been able to discover—in Charles Edward Smith's piece in *Symposium* of October 1930, in which he says that the Europeans "almost" beat out the Americans in the discovery of jazz.[7] Smith, in 1930, was not yet prepared to say that the Europeans had got there first: there was no evidence of it. But in September 1932, ironically, Rob Darrell wrote that, "British and Continental critics are intoxicated" by jazz and cited Goffin's *Music* and the British magazines *Rhythm* and the *Melody Maker* as examples of a more serious interest in jazz abroad.[8] (When reminded of this recently Darrell said, "Well, of course I wasn't thinking of my own writing.")[9]

But the primary responsibility for creating the myth of European priority in the appreciation of jazz was the American political left. According to S. Frederick Starr, in his important book *Red and Hot: The Fate of Jazz in the Soviet Union*, the Comintern decided in 1928 to treat American blacks as a "colonized nation." This "harebrained" policy, says Starr, was worked up by men "who had been no closer to America than the Lenin Library,"[10] but one corollary to it was the idea that jazz had to be seen as the "folk music" of this colonized race. After 1928 there was, then, an official attitude toward jazz on the left. It is not necessary to assume that the jazz fans who took up this view were all Communists: ideas of this kind circulated freely through people across the whole spectrum of left-wing philosophy.

One person who appears to have accepted this line of thought was John Hammond, rapidly becoming during the 1930s the most influential jazz writer in the world— indeed, perhaps the most influential critic the music has ever had. In the February 1932 issue of the *Melody Maker*, Hammond reported that Louis Armstrong had switched from Okeh Records, a minor label which aimed to a considerable extent at the black audience, to Victor, a major label. This move, Hammond said, attested to "the immense popularity of the great trumpet player."[11]

But by the next year Hammond had changed his mind about Armstrong's popularity. For the French magazine *Jazz Tango* he wrote, "The general public has never heard of" Armstrong.[12] For the *Melody Maker*'s audiences he said, "Although famous now in England, he is virtually unknown to the theatre public here."[13] (Hammond was not referring to the Broadway theater as we know it today, but to the vaudeville and movie houses where much jazz of the time was played.) Hammond clung to this later view right to the end of his life. Only a few years before he died he said that Armstrong was a "small cult figure" in this period and that "Even in the black areas they didn't know Louis. His records were never big sellers."[14]

This view cannot be supported. As early as the mid-1920s, according to William C. Parker, a student at Indiana University at the time, Armstrong's records were "very popular with small groups and the fraternity houses"[15]—and these were the early Hot Five records, not the much better-known big-band recordings of the period from 1929 on. By that year *Variety* said, "Three of Okeh's four hottest sellers are [by] Louis Armstrong's Savoy Ballroom Quintet."[16] In the fall of the same year, Armstrong was appearing in a hit play on Broadway and starring at Connie's Inn, one of the country's best-known cabarets.[17] In November 1930, *Variety* said that Armstrong was "hottest of the hot trumpeters, model of innumerable collegiate orchestras, a consistent recorder and good seller. . . ."[18] Rob Darrell reported that in 1930 Armstrong's records sold 100,000 copies, "without the aid of ballyhoo or high pressure distribution."[19]

What, then, caused Hammond to change his mind and start announcing that Armstrong was "unheard of" by general audiences in the United States?

John Hammond's parents were members of the American social elite, and were classic conservatives in most things. But Hammond's mother was also something of a reformer, a deeply religious woman with strong opinions. Hammond grew up with an instinctive sympathy for the underdog, and by the time he graduated from prep school, he was already inclining leftward in his political opinions. In December 1931, he reached the age of twenty-one and came into an unearned income of $12,000 a year, the sort of money only fairly important executives in business would make in the Depression year. He moved out of the family mansion into a small apartment in Greenwich Village.[20] The Bohemian artists and intellectuals he had chosen to live among were almost by reflex leftward. Many of them were ardent Socialists and at least some were members of the Communist party. Hammond was rebellious by nature, and he would not have easily put himself under the discipline of any established party line. But it is clear that he became, at this time, very sympathetic to the Communist viewpoint, at least in part because they seemed willing to support the cause of blacks, which Hammond was strongly interested in. It is fair, then, to infer from the timing of these events that in the months after Hammond left the family mansion to live in Greenwich Village, he had become politicized.

In later years, in his autobiography and other writings, he tended to slide over all of this, usually presenting himself as a man simply interested in social justice. There is little said about his left-wing affiliations in the autobiography—he leaves the impression that he wrote for left-wing magazines solely because they were the only papers that would give him space—and there is no mention in the liner notes for the recording of the 1938 "Spirituals to Swing" concert, issued much later, that the event was sponsored by the *New Masses*. But there can be no doubt that in the earlier day he supported the left in general and the Communist party in particular. Writing in the *Melody Maker* in December 1932, he said, "Come to think of it, the election is over. Tweedledum is replacing Tweedledee, and the Communists polled a bare 100,000. Such is America."[21] (Actually, the Communist party drew 102,785 votes and the various leftward parties combined drew more than a million, over three times the number they had drawn in the previous election,[22] suggesting a substantial upswing in popular support for the left, as was indeed the case.)

Hammond's writing, in general, followed this course. He wrote two excellent pieces for *The Nation* on the trial of the Scottsboro boys—some young black men who had been accused, apparently falsely, of raping two white women.[23] He vigorously attacked anti-union policies of the record companies in the *New Masses*.[24] Hammond's attacks on racism and exploitation of working people are much to his credit, and of course espousal of left-wing ideologies was commonplace among American intellectuals of the time. The problem is that he allowed his political views to temper his jazz writing. He was explicit about this. In a long piece criticizing Duke Ellington, he wrote that

. . . the real trouble with Duke's music is the fact that he has purposely kept himself from any contact with the troubles of his people or mankind in general. He consciously keeps himself from thinking about such problems as those of the southern sharecroppers, the Scottsboro boys, intolerable working and relief conditions in North and South.

According to Hammond, it was Ellington's lack of political fervor that had made his music "vapid and without the semblance of guts."[25]

Again, in the program notes for the aforementioned "Spirituals to Swing" concert, Hammond and his collaborator James Dugan said, speaking of black musicians, "The greatest of these artists die of privation and neglect and they are often found in the ironic situation of being world music idols and paupers at the same time."[26]

Hammond was hardly the only jazz critic of the period writing from a left-wing stance. Walter Schapp, a young jazz enthusiast of the period, said, "The American jazz fans all tended to be left wing."[27] Certainly Otis Ferguson, writing for the *New Republic*, was. Charles Edward Smith, had written for the *Daily Worker*, although he eventually wrote for *Time*—as many left-wingers of the day did. Rudi Blesh even adapted left-wing political terms to jazz criticism: New Orleans jazz was "collective" creation or improvisation; swing was "a reactionary music."[28] Indeed, one of the major American jazz clubs in the period, Cafe Society, was founded by left-wingers. According to the writer Helen Laurenson, the idea for the club came from the head of the American Communist party, Earl Browder, who saw it principally as a source of funds. Laurenson, who was interested in left-wing causes and did publicity for the club gratis, said that it had a "left-wing ambiance"; much of the comedy was social and political satire, and so was some of the music: Billie Holiday's celebrated *Strange Fruit*, about lynching, was created for Cafe Society audiences.[29] John Hammond was deeply involved with the club and was primarily responsible for choosing the musicians who played there. In sum, as Chris Albertson put it in his biography of Bessie Smith, the black musician

. . . became the darling of the late thirties' and early forties' left-wing liberal. Socialists and Communists found in America's black population the proletariat to suit their cause—what better way to show social concern than to have a "colored" man play for your gathering of friends?[30]

People like Rudi Blesh and Otis Ferguson were strong-minded, and did not need Hammond's help in forming political philosophies and opinions about jazz. Hammond, however, was by far the most widely published of these jazz writers from roughly 1935 to 1945. Such was his importance that profiles of him appeared in *Harper's*[31] and *Newsweek* which said that "on swing music he is an authority whose word is unquestioned.''[32] For better or worse, Hammond's opinions carried great weight with the more serious jazz fans who read about the music, not merely in the United States but in Europe as well; and it was his views, more than anybody else's, that impressed the jazz community.

At this late date it hardly matters who was and who was not following some putative party line. My point is simply that jazz had become, by the late 1930s, something of a left-wing cause. Hammond himself said:

> The people at the New Masses just hated jazz. But, since it was the days of the United Front and the days when they recorded blacks, they thought this would be good for their cultural image to have somebody write about jazz, particularly black jazz.[33]

I remember myself, as a boy growing up in a family with many left-wing—indeed, Communist party—connections, how frequently I could expect to find small collections of jazz records in the homes of my parents' friends.

In the 1920s, when jazz was arriving, American intellectuals were optimistic about the future of the country, which seemed to be filled with youth, energy, and excitement and was throwing up new art forms almost daily. In 1940, after ten years of a seemingly irreversible Depression, and with the dark shadow of fascism and world war looming, optimism was gone, and the United States no longer seemed to be the nation of the future. Now it seemed to be a corrupt and venal place where bloated plutocrats deliberately starved the families of coal-miners. The pendulum had swung with a vengeance. No longer was the United States the shining forward face of the world; that role now belonged to the U.S.S.R., where the great social experiment was going on. For these left-wing jazz writers, America was now the enemy, about which little good could be said. It followed, therefore, that the American bourgeoisie could not possibly have embraced jazz. The middle-class majority, as they saw it, was driven by material values to the exclusion of everything else, and could hardly appreciate the subtle beauties of jazz. This position almost forced these writers to see jazz as the music of the ghetto. This had not always been the view. Earlier jazz students had acknowledged that the music had come out of the black culture, as newspaper reports said again and again; but they believed, correctly or not, that, as R. D. Darrell put it, the music had "succeeded in assimilating whatever Negro, minstrel, semi-folk music, or other influences which went to make it up [and was] American to the core."

But now, in the late 1930s, America was not a very good place; jazz could not possibly be American to the core, but must surely be a music of the blacks—created by them, and played by them for their own pleasure in ghettos undisturbed by the white middle-class who hated the music, for racial reasons as much as anything.

For Hammond and other writers to believe this required them to deny a huge array of evidence to the contrary that was lying before their very eyes. In this period Louis Armstrong was making movies, playing major locations, recording, and broadcasting incessantly; Duke Ellington was grossing upwards of a million dollars a year, and his band was consistently being voted one of the top ones in the nation; Fats Waller was jiving for huge radio audiences, recording as many as forty sides a year, and appearing in major films; Billie Holiday was becoming celebrated and at least modestly wealthy; Count Basie and Jimmie Lunceford were leading two of the most popular bands in the country, and also becoming wealthy; a considerable number of other black musicians such as Art Tatum, Coleman Hawkins, and Roy Eldridge were earning more money than most white Americans; Bunny Berigan was a star soloist with Goodman, Dorsey, and his own band; and this says nothing about the raging success of the swing bands, which were making fortunes for Goodman, Miller, Woody Herman, and many more.

Nor were these jazz stars playing ghetto music. Ellington, Henderson, Lunceford, and many of the whites had come from middle-class families. Henderson was a college graduate with a degree in chemistry; and others, such as Lunceford and Hawkins, had had some college training.[34] More significantly, the jazz bands of the period were not, by and large, working in ghettos or playing for ghetto dwellers. The audience for their music was primarily, as it had always been, the white mainstream. All of the major jazz players of the time were playing frequently on college campuses, were having their records broadcast regularly on such popular radio shows as Martin Block's famous Make-Believe Ballroom, and were themselves often broadcasting live from theaters, hotels, and dance halls. To be sure, at times most of the black bands, at least, played black theaters and dances for sharecroppers in tobacco barns in the South, and their records were popular on juke boxes in Harlem and other black ghettos; but the jazz bands of the period were primarily part of a commercial entertainment industry whose function was to satisfy the general American public.

This conflict—between what actually was and what the writers saw—was cognitive dissonance of a high order. The writers were able to resolve it in part by reading out of jazz musicians who were popular with the public, especially if they were white. Many of the critics insisted that "swing," even when played by Duke Ellington, was commercial and therefore not jazz. John Hammond, who at the moment was pouring a lot of energy into promoting Count Basie, could not quite say that;

76

but he did say that Armstrong had been "corrupted . . . by ideas of chiseling managers"[35] and that Ellington was too arty.[36] There was a tendency for these writers to discover, and promote—sometimes wisely, sometimes not—black musicians whom they found playing for tips in black bars and southern juke joints. As a consequence there persists in jazz today a feeling that too much popularity is suspect, especially when white musicians are concerned.

But more than anything, these writers dealt with the gap between what was there and what they wanted to believe the way that human beings usually do in such cases—by carefully compartmentalizing what they knew from what they believed, so that the two were never in the same box, where the differences between them would be obvious.

Thus Marshall Stearns could write that the middle class remained "unmoved" by jazz, when he himself for decades had seen them cheering the music at places like the Cotton Club, the Famous Door, Cafe Society. Thus Hammond could say that black artists died in poverty and neglect in the very concert program that was being handed to members of the white middle class streaming into Carnegie Hall to see those neglected musicians perform. Thus Ferguson, Finkelstein, and others could insist that jazz was ghetto or folk music, when all of them were at that very moment, often as journalists, listening to major jazz musicians playing in fancy ballrooms and big city theaters. Indeed, at times some of these writers seem, almost to be deliberately thumbing their noses at the facts. As recently as 1987 Leonard Feather wrote that jazz was "belittled or ignored or condescended to for half a century by most white Americans," and he went on to make the astonishing statement that it was "long forbidden in colleges where there were severe penalties for practising it."[37] College campuses were of course the section of American society most receptive to jazz, with Oliver, Ory, and the Original Dixieland Jass Band playing regularly at college dances from the time of World War I, and students organizing jazz bands on dozens of campuses from the early 1920s right up to today.

Unfortunately, some of these writers took it a step further, and allowed themselves to say things that they could not have believed. Rudi Blesh could not have believed that blacks had to play with their faces to the wall; he was an authority on New Orleans jazz, and if he had been told so bizarre a story he could easily have checked it with the New Orleans musicians he knew. Hammond could not have believed that jazz was looked on with "horror" by club managers in the 1920s; he knew many of them personally, and had seen club after club reaching out for musicians who could play the popular new music.

But those who were deliberately falsifying the historical record were, I think, in the minority. For most it was simply that they wanted to believe that Americans disliked jazz, and were able to suspend disbelief sufficiently to do so. So we have writers saying that little jazz was recorded in the United States during the early 1930s, when their own works are studded with references to the classics of the period. So we have writers insisting that jazz was ignored by white Americans in the early days, when their own books are filled with stories of whites flooding into Harlem in the 1920s and reports of Henderson, Ellington, and others making long stands at famous white-only cabarets and dance halls. So we have writers of books on Ellington saying that he was nurtured by Europeans, when their own books show that Ellington made only two brief trips to Europe in the first fifty years of his life, and his audience to that point was almost entirely white Americans. Such examples could be multiplied indefinitely.

There is, of course, no reason why Europeans should have been expected to have taken to jazz as Americans did. Americans, after all, had begun hearing quantities of black music as early as the 1830s, when the so-called plantation songs, with their syncopations and dotted rhythms, became popular. They were later washed by a flood of minstrel music, and then spirituals derived from black gospel music. Finally there came ragtime, a major element in popular music after 1900, and somewhat later the first blues. Jazz came as no surprise to Americans, who found it another step in a direction they had long been travelling. Europeans, lacking a large black sub-culture in their midst, did not have the same cultural experience and could hardly be expected to have accepted jazz in the easy way that Americans did when it first came to their attention at the time of World War I.

It is obvious that we cannot really know a cultural artifact without understanding its relationship to the culture from which it sprang. Otis Ferguson said in 1939 that jazz, "has been a national institution for twenty years."[38] He was absolutely correct, and in order to know what jazz really is, we cannot continue to see it as an outcast in America. We must see that it evolved as it did *because* of majority attitudes, not in spite of them. Nor for that matter can we really understand the United States if we continue to insist that one of its most famous creations was despised by the culture as a whole. For jazz, I believe, represents much that is best about America: the frankness and generosity that have always been thought to be characteristic of its people; the freedom of expression that is built into its Constitution; and the spontaneity that is so crucial a part of the music. In sum, what is essential to jazz is precisely the Americanism that lies at its heart; and what is typical of America is this jazz music that is produced and nurtured.

NOTES

Chapter I

[1] Neil Leonard, *Jazz and the White Americans* (Chicago: University of Chicago Press, 1962), p. 2.

[2] Sidney Finkelstein, *Jazz: A People's Music* (New York: Citadel Press, 1948; repr. New York: Da Capo Press, 1975), p. 127.

[3] Whitney Balliett, *American Musicians: Fifty-Six Portraits in Jazz* (New York: Oxford University Press, 1986). p. 3.

[4] Frank Tirro, *Jazz: A History* (New York: W. W. Norton, 1977), p. 155.

[5] Rudi Blesh, *Shining Trumpets: A History of Jazz* (New York: Alfred A. Knopf, 1946; repr. New York: Da Capo Press, 1975), p. 3.

[6] Marshall Stearns, *The Story of Jazz* (New York: Oxford University Press, 1956; repr. 1973), p. 191.

[7] Leroy Ostransky, *Understanding Jazz* (Englewood Cliffs, NJ: Prentice-Hall, 1977), pp. 4, 17.

[8] *New Masses* 18/10 (3 March 1936), 27–28.

[9] Program of the concert "Spirituals to Swing," Carnegie Hall, New York, 23 December 1938.

[10] Author's interview, 1982.

[11] *Down Beat* (1 May 1940), p. 19.

[12] *Jazz Times* (April 1985), p. 11.

[13] Balliett, *American Musicians*, p. 3.

[14] Derek Jewell, *Duke: A Portrait of Duke Ellington* (New York: W. W. Norton, 1977), p. 120.

[15] *Down Beat* (1 May 1940), p. 6.

[16] Peter Gammond, *Duke Ellington: His Life and Music* (London: Phoenix House; repr. New York: Da Capo Press, 1977), p. 134.

[17] Author's interview, 1982.

[18] Francis Newton [Eric Hobsbawm], *The Jazz Scene* (New York: Monthly Review Press, 1960; repr. New York: Da Capo Press, 1975), pp. 239, 64.

[19] Robert Goffin, *Jazz: From the Congo to the Metropolitan* (Garden City, NY: Doubleday, 1944; repr. New York: Da Capo Press, 1975), p. 83.

[20] Ian Carr, *Miles Davis* (New York: William Morrow, 1982), p. 41.

[21] John Hammond, "American News," *Melody Maker* 8/85 (January 1933), 23.

[22] Timme Rosenkrantz, "Reflections on Louis Armstrong," *Down Beat* 29/20 (19 July 1962), 50.

[23] Blesh, *Shining Trumpets*, p. 8.

[24] *Jazz Forum* (1987/2), p. 31.

[25] Herbert G. Gutman, *The Black Family in Slavery and Freedom, 1750–1925* (New York: Pantheon Books, 1976), p. 389.

[26] See respectively Willie (the Lion) Smith with George Hoefer, *Music on My Mind* (Garden City, NY: Doubleday, 1964); repr. New York: Da Capo Press, 1975), pp. 45–46; Tom Stoddard, *Jazz on the Barbary Coast* (Chigwell, England: Storyville Publications, 1982), p. 10; Al Rose, *Storyville, New Orleans* (University: University of Alabama Press, 1974), p. 169; and Illinois-Chicago Commission on Race Relations, *The Negro in Chicago* (New York: Arno Press and the New York Times, 1968), pp. 323–24.

[27] Quoted in Balliett, *American Musicians*, p. 84.

[28] Stoddard, *Jazz on the Barbary Coast*, p. 96.

[29] "Small's Paradise," *Variety* 83 (26 May 1926), 50.

[30] Eileen Southern, *The Music of Black Americans: A History*, 2d ed. (New York: W. W. Norton, 1983), pp. 50–53.

[31] Robert C. Toll, *Blacking Up: The Minstrel Show in Nineteenth-Century America* (New York: Oxford University Press, 1974), p. 195.

[32] Thomas L. Riis, "Black Musical Theatre in New York, 1890–1915" (Ph.D. dissertation, University of Michigan, 1981), p. 139.

[33] Oral history of Tom Whaley (no. 3, p. 59), Institute of Jazz Studies, Rutgers University (hereafter cited as Rutgers archives).

[34] *Billboard* (14 March 1925), p. 53.

[35] Personal communication, New Orleans, 24 January 1987.

[36] Pops Foster, as told to Tom Stoddard, *The Autobiography of Pops Foster* (Berkeley: University of California Press, 1971), p. 65.

[37] Oral history of Hyppolite Charles, William Hogan Ransom Archive of Jazz, Tulane University (hereafter cited as Tulane archives).

[38] Personal communication from Curt Jerde, director of the Tulane archives. Jerde has seen reports in Tulane student newspapers of "Orry's band" playing subscription dances in the university gymnasium.

[39] Oral history of Stella Oliver, Tulane archives.

[40] Nat Shapiro and Nat Hentoff, *Hear Me Talkin' to Ya* (New York: Rinehart, 1955; repr. New York: Dover Publications, 1966), p. 17.

[41] Foster, *Autobiography*, p. 108.

[42] *New Orleans Times-Picayune*, 20 June 1918.

[43] Letters of 2 July and 29 June 1918 in the *Times-Picayune* (clippings in the Nick LaRocca scrapbooks, Tulane archives).

[44] Stoddard, *Jazz on the Barbary Coast*, p. 147.

[45] Mrs. Vernon Castle, *My Husband* (New York: C. Scribner's Sons, 1919; repr. New York: Da Capo Press, 1979), p. 53.

[46] H. O. Brunn, *The Story of the Original Dixieland Jazz Band* (Baton Rouge: Louisiana State University Press, 1960), chap. 3.

[47] *Billboard* (1 September 1916); unpaged clipping in Nick LaRocca scrapbooks, Tulane archives.

[48] Oral history of Nick LaRocca, Tulane archives.

[49] *New York Sun*, 4 November 1917.

[50] Oral history of Lewis Metcalf (C-467), Schomburg Center for Research in Black Culture, New York City.

[51] Undated clipping in Nick LaRocca scrapbooks, Tulane archives.

[52] *Variety* (March 1917); otherwise undated clipping in Nick LaRocca scrapbooks, Tulane archives.

[53] *The Dance* (December 1917), p. 7.

[54] See in particular Shapiro and Hentoff, *Hear Me Talkin'*, pp. 115–27.

[55] James Lincoln Collier, *Louis Armstrong: American Genius* (New York: Oxford University Press, 1983), p. 70.

[56] Among material in the Nick LaRocca scrapbooks, Tulane archives.

[57] *Living Age* (31 July 1920), p. 280.

[58] Robert J. Cole, "Conspiracy of Silence Against Jazz," *New York Times*, 21 September 1919, sec. 7.

[59] *New York American*, 18 November 1917.

[60] Unidentified clipping in Nick LaRocca scrapbooks, Tulane archives.

[61] *New York Sun*, 4 November 1917 (cliping in Nick LaRocca scrapbooks, Tulane archives).

[62] "A Negro Explains Jazz," *Literary Digest* 61/4 (26 April 1919), 28–29.

[63] Clipping in Nick LaRocca scrapbooks, Tulane archives.

Chapter II

[1] Collier, *Louis Armstrong*, chaps. 8, 13,

[2] Oral history of John Hammond, Oral History American Music, Yale University (hereafter cited as Yale archives), p. 29; Smith with Hoefer, *Music on My Mind*, pp. 136–37.

[3] Shapiro and Hentoff, *Hear Me Talkin'*, p. 126.

[4] Dempsey J. Travis, *An Autobiography of Black Jazz* (Chicago: Urban Research Institute, 1983), p. 324.

[5] Ibid.

[6] Collier, *Louis Armstrong*, p. 94.

[7] *Billboard* (14 July 1923), p. 51.

[8] The Music Research Division, New York Public Library at Lincoln Center, has a collection of these catalogues.

[9] Author's interview with Sherwood Mangiapane, New Orleans, fall 1981.

[10] Erik Barnouw, *A Tower of Babel: A History of Broadcasting in the United States* (New York: Oxford University Press, 1966), I, 130.

[11] Stanley Dance, *The World of Duke Ellington* (New York: Charles Scribner's Sons, 1970), p. 120.

[12] Note (probably by George Hoefer) from interview in Lil Hardin Armstrong folder, vertical file, Rutgers archives.

[13] *Vanity Fair* (August 1925), p. 57.

[14] Lewis A Ehrenberg, *Steppin' Out* (Westport, CT: Greenwood Press, 1981), p. xiii.

[15] Edmund Wilson, *The Fifties* (New York: Farrar, Straus & Giroux, 1986), p. xxii.

[16] *Musical Courier* (11 May 1922), p. 6.

[17] *The Nation* (25 October 1922), p. 438.

[18] See especially J. A. Jackson's columns in *Billboard*, in 1923–25.

[19] E. Sparling, "Ghost Writer of Jazz," *Scribner's* 90 (December 1931), 594–600.

[20] David Ewen, *Men of Popular Music* (Chicago and New York: Ziff-Davis, 1944), pp. 93–96.

[21] Ibid.

[22] Thomas A. DeLong, *Pops* (Piscataway, NJ: New Century Publishers, 1983), pp. 15–18.

[23] *Scribner's* 90 (December 1931), 594.

[24] *American Mercury* (26 April 1927), p. 385.

[25] *Scribner's* 90 (December 1931), 594.

[26] Charles Schwartz, *Gershwin: His Life and Music* (Indianapolis: Bobbs-Merrill, 1973; repr. New York: Da Capo Press, 1979), p. 70; *Literary Digest* (24 November 1923), p. 31.

[27] *New York Times Book Review and Magazine* (19 February 1922), p. 8.

[28] H. O. Osgood, "Anatomy of Jazz," *American Mercury* (26 April 1927), pp. 385–95.

[29] *Popular Mechanics*, ca. 1922 (undated clipping in Nick LaRocca scrapbooks, Tulane archives).

[30] *The Clipper* (8 November 1922), p. 28.

[31] Ibid. (15 November 1922), p. 28.

[32] *Billboard* (14 February 1925), p. 20.

[33] *The Clipper* (10 April 1924), p. 14.

[34] *Billboard* (15 September 1923), p. 52; (27 October 1923), p. 54; (1 November 1924), p. 48; (31 January 1925), p. 50.

[35] *Billboard* (17 January 1925).

[36] Ibid. (31 January 1925), p. 50.

[37] *Orchestra World* (October 1925), p. 11. The following four references come from the issues of February 1926, September 1926, November 1926, and January 1927, respectively.

[38] Ibid., issues in the spring of 1931.

[39] Leonard, *Jazz and the White Americans*, p. 89.

[40] *Melody Maker* (January 1931), p. 33.

[41] James Lincoln Collier, *Duke Ellington* (New York: Oxford University Press, 1987), p. 101.

[42] *Orchestra World* (May 1931), p. 5.

[43] Oral history of Bud Freeman, Rutgers archives (no. 2, p. 20).

[44] Shapiro and Hentoff, *Hear Me Talkin'*, p. 281.

[45] *American Mercury* (26 April 1927), p. 388.

[46] *Orchestra World* (October 1925), p. 1.

[47] *Melody Maker* (January 1931), p. 33.

[48] *The Clipper* (15 May 1924).

[49] Al Rose and Edmond Souchon, *New Orleans Jazz* (Baton Rouge: Louisiana State University Press, 1984), p. 266.

[50] Oral history of Jimmy McPartland, Rutgers archives (no. 1, p. 51).

[51] Recordings by the last three of these bands have been reissued as *The College Bands, 1925–30* (Sunbeam MFC-21).

[52] Author's interview with Francis (Cork) O'Keefe, 23 February 1983.

[53] Herb Sanford, *Tommy & Jimmy Dorsey: The Dorsey Years* (New York: Arlington House, 1972; repr. New York: Da Capo Press, 1980), p. 39.

[54] *Variety* (28 December 1927), p. 47, as quoted in Walter C. Allen, *Hendersoniana* (Highland Park, NJ: Walter C. Allen, 1973), p. 218.

[55] Ibid.

[56] Ibid., p. 227.

[57] *Disques* (September 1932), p. 290.

[58] Collier, *Louis Armstrong*, p. 131.

[59] Collier, *Duke Ellington*, p. 100

[60] *Variety* (9 May 1928), p. 119.

[61] See Allen, *Hendersoniana*, for these and other details of Henderson's career.

[62] Collier, *Duke Ellington*, pp. 45, 77.

[63] Collier, *Louis Armstrong*, chaps. 10, 13.

[64] Stanley Dance, *The World of Earl Hines* (New York: Scribner's, 1977), p. 49.

[65] On Ory, see *Record Changer* (November 1947); on Smith, see *Billboard* (14 July 1923), p. 51.

[66] Ethel Waters and Charles Samuels, *His Eye is on the Sparrow* (Garden City, NY: Doubleday, 1950), p. 158.

[67] Allen, *Hendersoniana*, p. 90.

[68] Barnouw, *A Tower of Babel*, p. 130.

[69] *Melody Maker* (September 1932), p. 749.

[70] Stearns, *The Story of Jazz*, p. 180.

[71] DeLong, *Pops*, p. 124.

[72] In the *Melody Maker* (September 1932), p. 749.

[73] *Jazz Educators' Journal* (February–March 1986), p. 10.

[74] *Billboard* (7 June 1924), p. 2.

[75] *Jazz Educators' Journal* (February–March 1986), p. 11.

[76] Leonard, *Jazz and the White Americans*, p. 139.

[77] *Down Beat* (February 1936), p. 1.

[78] Benny Goodman scrapbooks, John Herrick Jackson Music Library, Yale University.

[79] Otherwise unidentified clipping in Benny Goodman scrapbooks, John Herrick Jackson Music Library, Yale University.

[80] James Lincoln Collier, *The Making of Jazz* (Boston: Houghton Mifflin, 1978), pp. 292ff.

[81] Lewis Porter, *Lester Young* (Boston: Twayne Publishers, 1985), p. 26.

[82] Collier, *The Making of Jazz*, p. 486.

[83] Ralph J. Gleason, "Critic Demands Junking of Weakling Jazzmen," *Down Beat* 20/24 (2 December 1953), 2.

[84] Ralph Ellison, *Shadow and Act* (New York: Random House, 1964), p. 228.

[85] *Jazz Forum* 103, p. 21.

Chapter III

[1] Henry Edward Krehbiel, *Afro-American Folksong: A Study in Racial and National Music* (New York: G. Schirmer, 1914).

[2] Virgil Thomson, "The Future of American Music," *Vanity Fair* (September 1925), p. 62.

[3] Charles Peabody, "Notes on Negro Music," *Journal of American Folklore* 16/62 (July–September 1903), 148–52.

[4] See in particular Shapiro and Hentoff, *Hear Me Talkin'*.

[5] R. D. Darrell, "All Quiet on the Western Jazz Front," *Disques* 3/7 (September 1932), pp. 290–94.

[6] John Hammond, "The Sad Case of Louis Armstrong," *Jazz Tango*, No. 34 (July 1933), p. 17.

86

7 Figure provided by Sterling Library, Yale University.

8 Thomas D. Snyder, *Digest of Education Statistics* (Washington, DC: Center for Education Statistics, United States Government Printing Office, 1987), p. 121.

9 "Hot Record Society," *Time* (17 May 1937), p. 50.

10 "The Appeal of the Primitive Jazz," *Literary Digest* 55 (25 August 1917), 28–29. It is not clear whether the quoted phrase originated with Patterson and is quoted by Kingsley, or with Kingsley himself. My judgment is that the analysis was made by Patterson.

11 Respectively *The Review* (24 May 1919); J. Schultz, "Jazz," *The Nation* 115 (25 October 1922), 438–39; G. Seldes, "Toujours Jazz," *The Dial* 75 (August 1923), 151–66; *New York Times*, 2 September 1919, sec. 7, p. 6; *New York Times*, 18 December 1921, Sunday Magazine, p. 3; and *New York Times*, 25 June 1922, sec. 3, p. 8.

12 "Jazz: A Musical Discussion," *The Atlantic* 130 (August 1922), 182–89.

13 "Where is Jazz Leading America?," *The Etude* 42 (August–September 1924), 517–18, 595–96.

14 *New York Times*, 13 February 1924.

15 Virgil Thomson, "Enter: American-Made Music," *Vanity Fair* 25/2 (October 1925), 71, 124.

16 *New York Times*, 26 September 1926, sec. 4, p. 2.

17 "Blue Notes," *New Republic* 45/583 (3 February 1926), 292–93.

18 Ibid.

19 "A Negro Explains Jazz"; Virgil Thomson, "Jazz," *American Mercury* 2 (August 1924), 465–67.

20 C. F. Smith, "Jazz: Some Little-Known Aspects," *The Symposium* 1/4 (October 1930), 513.

21 Otherwise unidentified clipping, vertical file, Rutgers archives.

22 See Bruce Kellner, *Carl Van Vechten and the Irreverent Decades* (Norman: University of Oklahoma Press, 1968), passim.

23 "The Black Blues," *Vanity Fair* 24/6 (August 1925), 57.

24 *Vanity Fair* 25/2 (October 1925), 46.

25 *Vanity Fair* 24/6 (August 1925), 86, 92.

[26] Author's interviews with Darrell, 21 May 1982, 4 October 1984 (as also for the material in the following paragraph).

[27] *Phonograph Monthly Review* 1/1 (October 1926), 9.

[28] Ibid. 1/8 (May 1927), 364.

[29] Ibid. 1/10 (July 1927), 413.

[30] Ibid. 1/12 (September 1927), 498.

[31] Ibid. 4/10 (July 1930), 358.

[32] Ibid. 5/2 (November 1930), 69.

[33] Ibid. 5/3 (December 1930), 102.

[34] Ibid. 6/5 (February 1932), 99.

[35] Ibid. 5/12 (September 1931), 336.

[36] Ibid. 5/4 (January 1931), 137.

[37] Ibid. 5/9 (June 1931), 274.

[38] *Disques* 6/9 (June 1932), 153–57.

[39] Carol J. Oja, "R. D. Darrell, A Pioneer in American Music," *I.S.A.M. Newsletter* 15/2 (May 1986), 14–15.

[40] Author's interviews with Darrell, and letter from Darrell to Ellington of 26 March 1932 (copy in author's file).

[41] Edmund Wilson, "Night Clubs," *New Republic* 44/562 (9 September 1925), 71.

[42] Newton [Hobsbawm], *The Jazz Scene*, p. 246.

[43] Ibid., p. 64.

Chapter IV

[1] *The Star* (London), 19 April 1919.

[2] *Melody Maker* 10/54 (2 June 1934), 8. The author of the article, Lew Davis, had attended the show.

[3] *Orchestra World* (January 1926), p. 19.

[4] *New York Times*, 31 May 1924, sec. 1, p. 2.

[5] *Orchestra World* (January 1927), p. 7.

[6] *New York Times*, 11 December 1924, sec. 2, p. 5.

[7] See especially Chris Goddard, *Jazz Away from Home* (London: Paddington Press, 1979), and Jim Godbolt, *A History of Jazz in Britain* (London: Quartet, 1984), for discussions of tours by American musicians in the 1920s.

[8] Author's interviews with the English musicians Harry Lewis and Harry Gold, spring 1982.

[9] This judgment is based on study of recordings of early jazz played in England, Germany, Belgium, France, and the U.S.S.R., compiled by authorities on the respective local jazz scenes, including *Jazz in Deutschland, 1912–1928* (EMI Lc 134–32 447/8); *Anthology of Soviet Jazz: the First Steps* (Melodiya M60 45827 006); *Charles Remue and his New Stompers Orchestra—1929* (Retrieval FG-401); Le Jazz en France, vol. 9: *Pionniers du jazz français 1906–31*; and *A Word from the English* (Sunbeam MFC-2).

[10] *The Times* (London), 26 September 1927, p. 8.

[11] Sid Colin, *And the Bands Played On* (London: Elm Tree Books, 1977), p. 36.

[12] *Orchestra World* (January 1927), p. 3.

[13] Colin, *And the Bands Played On*, p. 45.

[14] Godbolt, *A History of Jazz in Britain*, p. 61.

[15] Oral history of Max Jones, Yale archives (no. 557, p. 5).

[16] Bert Ralton, "The Original Havana Band," *Melody Maker* 2/1 (February 1926), 29.

[17] 'Needlepoint,' "The Gramophone Review," *Melody Maker* 2/13 (January 1927), 43–47.

[18] Ibid. (December 1928).

[19] 'Needlepoint,' "The Gramophone Review," *Melody Maker* 2/18 (June 1927), 573.

[20] Fred and "Lizz" Elizalde, "Who's Who in American Bands," *Melody Maker* 2/17 (May 1927), 419, 421.

[21] Clive Bell, "Plus de Jazz," *New Republic* 28/355 (21 September 1921), 92–96.

[22] *Life and Letters* 1/2 (July 1928), 125–26.

[23] André Coeuroy and André Schaeffner, *Le jazz* (Paris: Editions Claude Aveline, 1926), pp. 103–5.

[24] *La nouvelle revue* (15 June 1931), p. 295.

[25] *New York Times*, 4 September 1932, sec. 6, p. 1.

[26] Author's interview with Delaunay, Paris, March 1975.

[27] Hugues Panassié, *Douze années de jazz* (Paris: Editions Corréa, 1946), p. 12.

[28] Irving Schwerké, *Kings Jazz and David* (Paris: Les Presses Modernes, 1927), p. 34.

[29] Oral history of Bud Freeman, Rutgers archives (no. 2, p. 56).

[30] Robert Pernet, *Jazz in Little Belgium 1881–1966* (Brussels: Sigma, 1967), pp. 93–96.

[31] *Jazz Forum* 101 (1986).

[32] "New York—Its Dance Music and Musicians," *Melody Maker* 4/47 (November 1929), 1027–30.

[33] Panassié, *Douze années de jazz*, p. 12.

[34] *Le jazz hot* (Paris: Editions Corréa, 1934); *Hot Jazz* (New York: M. Witmark and Sons, 1936).

[35] *Melody Maker* (22 July 1933), quoted in Godbolt, *A History of Jazz in Britain*, p. 115.

[36] Colin, *And the Bands Played On*, p. 101.

[37] *Melody Maker* 10/67 (1 September 1934), 1.

[38] *Down Beat* (October 1935), p. 3.

[39] *Down Beat* (26 August 1946), p. 4.

[40] Author's interview with Harry Lewis (who was in London in the 1930s), spring 1982.

[41] *Down Beat* (26 August 1946), p. 4.

[42] *Down Beat* (6 April 1951), p. 1.

[43] *Down Beat* (25 February 1953), p. 6, 16.

[44] My discussion of jazz activity in Europe in recent years is based on some twenty trips there, including residencies in England and France, during which I visited almost all the European countries, including Russia and others in the Eastern bloc, and in most cases held lengthy conversations with leading jazz musicians, critics, and promoters about conditions for jazz in their countries. The better-known among these included: from England, John Chilton and Sinclair Traill; from France, Charles Delaunay and Maurice Culloz; from Germany, Joachim Berendt and Albert Mangelsdorf; from Portugal, José Duarte and Luis Villas Boas; from Italy, Carlo Loffredo; from Greece, Sakis Papadimitriou and Kostas Yiannoulopoulos; from Yugoslavia, Dusan Latkovic and Nikola Mitrovic; from Poland, Pawel Brodowski and Zbigniew Namyslowski; from Hungary, Imre Kiss; from Czechoslovakia, Emil Viklicky; from Bulgaria, Vladimir Gadzhev and Vladimir Dmitrov; from the U.S.S.R., Vyacheslav Ganelin, Oleg Lundstrem, Alexey Batshev, and Georgi Bacjiev. I have also had the privilege of "sitting in" with local bands in London and elsewhere in England, and in Paris, Budapest, Leningrad, Zurich, and Munich.

[45] *Jazzletter* 6/9 (September 1987), 6.

Chapter V

[1] "Hot Record Society," *Time* (17 May 1937), p. 50.

[2] *New York Review of Books* (26 March 1987), p. 53.

[3] Sidney Bechet, *Treat It Gentle: An Autobiography* (New York: Farrar, Straus & Giroux, 1960; repr. New York: Da Capo Press, 1978), p. 12.; Godbolt, *A History of Jazz in Britain*, p. 16; Goddard, *Jazz Away from Home*, p. 59; Gunther Schuller, *Early Jazz: Its Roots and Musical Development* (New York: Oxford University Press, 1968), p. 195.

[4] See Chapter III, n. 10.

[5] See Chapter IV, n. 23.

[6] A. Baresel, *Das Jazz-Buch* (Leipzig: Jul. Heins. Zimmerman, 1926).

[7] E. F. Burian, *Jazz* (Prague, 1928). A discussion of this work appears in *Jazz Forum* 101 (1986).

[8] Paul Whiteman and Mary Margaret McBride, *Jazz* (New York: J. H. Sears & Co., 1926).

[9] Henry O. Osgood, *So This is Jazz* (Boston: Little, Brown and Co., 1926).

[10] J. Peter Burkholder, *Charles Ives: the Ideas Behind the Music* (New Haven, CT: Yale University Press, 1985), pp. 66–67.

[11] H. Wiley Hitchcock, *Music in the United States*, rev. 3d ed. (Englewood Cliffs, NJ: Prentice-Hall, 1988), p. 190.

[12] Thomson, "Enter: American-Made Music."

[13] Goffin, *Jazz: From the Congo to the Metropolitan*, p. 2.

[14] Goffin, *Aux frontières du jazz* (Paris: Editions du Sagittaire, 1932).

[15] Goffin, *Aux frontières du jazz*, p. 87.

[16] Ibid., p. 44.

[17] Ibid.

[18] Ibid., p. 47.

[19] Ibid., p. 100.

[20] Ibid., passim.

[21] 'Mike' [Patrick "Spike" Hughes], "Gramophone Review," *Melody Maker* 7/83 (November 1932), 927–35.

[22] Ibid., 6/67 (July 1931), 573–81.

[23] 'Mike,' "Five Good Records," *Melody Maker* 10/69 (November 1934), 5.

[24] Leonard Hibbs, ed., *A Short Survey of Modern Rhythm on Brunswick Records* (London: Published in conjunction with the Brunswick Record Co., 1934).

[25] Ibid., p. 6.

[26] *The Bookman* (January 1929), p. 571.

[27] Darrell, "All Quiet on the Western Jazz Front."

[28] "Black Beauty," *Disques* 3/4 (June 1932), 152–61.

[29] Goddard, *Jazz Away from Home*, p. 141.

[30] Copies of *Rhythm, Orkester Journalen*, and *Hot News* are available in the Rutgers archives.

[31] Hugues Panassié, "Louis Armstrong," *Jazz Tango* 1/3–4 (25 December 1930), 7.

[32] Hugues Panassié, "Muggsy Spanier," *Jazz Tango* 2/5 (February 1931), 5–6.

[33] Hugues Panassié, "Jack Teagarden," *Jazz Tango* 2/7 (April 1931), [3]-[4].

[34] Hugues Panassié, "Les grands trombones hot," *Jazz Tango* 2/8 (May 1931), 4.

[35] Hugues Panassié, "Bix Beiderbecke," *Jazz Tango* 2/13 (October 1931), 7.

[36] Dance, *The World of Earl Hines*, p. 48.

[37] *Chicago Defender*, 10 August 1929.

[38] *Variety* 100 (12 November 1930), 73.

[39] *Melody Maker* (March 1930)

[40] Hugues Panassié, *Hot Jazz: The Guide to Swing Music* (New York: M. Witmark and Sons, 1936), p. 25.

[41] Ibid., p. 38.

[42] Ibid., p. 56.

[43] Ibid., p. 65.

[44] Ibid., p. 66.

[45] Ibid., p. 52.

[46] Dorothy Chamberlain and Robert Wilson, eds., *The Otis Ferguson Reader* (Highland Park, IL: December Press, 1982), p. 186.

[47] Frederic Ramsey, Jr., and Charles Edward Smith, eds., *Jazzmen* (New York: Harcourt, Brace, 1939; repr. New York: Harvest/HBJ, 1977), p. 103.

[48] Finkelstein, *Jazz*, p. 3.

[49] Letter to Ronald G. Welburn, 31 August 1982, photoreproduced in Welburn, "American Jazz Criticism, 1914-1940" (Ph.D. dissertation, New York University, 1983), pp. 189-90.

[50] Winthrop Sargeant, *Jazz, Hot and Hybrid* (New York: E. P. Dutton, 1938; rev. and enl. ed. 1946; repr. with additions New York: Da Capo Press, 1975).

[51] Wilder Hobson, *American Jazz Music* (New York: W. W. Norton, 1939; repr. New York: Da Capo Press, 1976).

[52] Goffin, *Aux frontières du jazz*, p. 45. Goffin cites a *Literary Digest* article of 25 August 1917, and internal evidence suggests he saw at least one other one.

[53] Interview with Hammond conducted and transcribed by Ronald G. Welburn, in Welburn, "American Jazz Criticism," pp. 206–15; this quotation is from p. 213.

[54] Balliett, *American Musicians*, p. 10.

[55] Ibid., p. 7.

[56] Ibid.

[57] Ibid., p. 4.

[58] Andrew Motion, *The Lamberts: George, Constant & Kit* (New York: Farrar, Straus & Giroux, 1987), p. 13.

[59] Ibid., pp. 174, 186.

[60] Ibid., p. 135.

[61] Hibbs, ed., *A Short Survey*, p. 4; *Disques* 1/2 (February 1931), 535.

[62] Letter from Edgar Jackson to R. D. Darrell of 27 September 1932 (in author's file).

[63] Peter Gammond, ed., *Duke Ellington: His Life and Music* (London: Phoenix House, 1958; repr. New York: Da Capo Press, 1977), p. 87; Jewell, *Duke*, pp. 55–56; Collier, *Duke Ellington*, p. 158.

[64] Roland Gelatt, *The Fabulous Phonograph* (New York: Collier Books, 1977), p. 255.

[65] Shapiro and Hentoff, *Hear Me Talkin'*, pp. 196–97.

[66] Bechet, *Treat It Gentle*, p. 159.

[67] Jim Haskins, *The Cotton Club* (New York: New American Library, 1977), pp. 81–82.

[68] My estimate, based on the listings in Brian Rust, *Jazz Records 1897–1942* (Chigwell, England: Storyville Publications, 1975).

[69] Collier, *Louis Armstrong*, p. 255.

[70] Stearns, *The Story of Jazz*, p. v.

[71] Blesh, *Shining Trumpets*, p. 158.

[72] Beginning with articles in *The Nation* (20 December 1933), p. 465; (26 April 1933). p. 701.

[73] *American Music Lover* 1/5 (September 1935), 158.

[74] C. L. Cons, "Jargon of Jazz," *American Mercury* 38/sup. 10 (May 1936); Reed Dickerson, "Hot Music," *Harper's* (April 1936), 567–74; H. L. Kaufman, "From Ragtime to Swing," *Scholastic* 29–30 (30 April 1938), and "Round and Round," *Literary Digest* 26 (4 April 1936).

[75] Described in the article cited in this section, n. 1.

Chapter VI

[1] *Chicago Defender*, 9 July 1921, p. 7.

[2] Collier, *Louis Armstrong*, p. 254.

[3] Barry Ulanov, *Duke Ellington* (New York: Creative Age Press, 1946), pp. 133–34.

[4] Christopher Collier and James Lincoln Collier, *Decision in Philadelphia* (New York: Random House/Reader's Digest Press, 1986), p. 67.

[5] Malcolm Cowley, *Exile's Return* (New York: Viking Press, 1956), p. 106.

[6] *Dreiser-Mencken Letters: The Correspondence of Theodore Dreiser and H. L. Mencken 1907–1945*, ed. Thomas P. Riggio (Philadelphia: University of Pennsylvania Press, 1986), pp. 396–97, 371.

[7] *Symposium* 1/4 (October 1930), 502–17.

[8] Darrell, "All Quiet on the Western Jazz Front."

[9] Private communication by telephone, August 1987.

[10] S. Frederick Starr, *Red and Hot: The Fate of Jazz in the Soviet Union* (New York: Oxford University Press, 1983), pp. 101–2.

[11] John H. Hammond, Jr., "American News," *Melody Maker* 7/74 (February 1932), 151.

[12] *Jazz Tango* 34 (July 1933), 17.

[13] John H. Hammond, Jr., "American News," *Melody Maker* 8/85 (January 1933), 23.

[14] Author's interview with Hammond, 1982.

[15] Author's interview with Parker, 1979.

[16] *Variety* (3 April 1929), p. 64.

[17] For details of Armstrong's career, see Collier, *Louis Armstrong*.

[18] *Variety* (12 November 1930), p. 73.

[19] *Disques* (September 1932), p. 291.

[20] John Hammond with Irving Townsend, *John Hammond on Record* (New York: Summit Books, 1977), pp. 16–18, 65–68.

[21] John H. Hammond, Jr., "American News," *Melody Maker* 7/84 (December 1932), 1056.

[22] Richard Hofstadter, William Miller, and Daniel Aaron, *The American Republic* (Englewood Cliffs, NJ: Prentice-Hall, 1959), 2:698.

[23] *The Nation* 137 (26 April 1933), 701; 137 (20 December 1933), 465.

[24] Henry Johnson [John H. Hammond, Jr.], "Music," *New Masses* (31 March 1936), p. 27; (14 April 1936), p. 29; (28 April 1936), p. 29.

[25] *Down Beat* (6 November 1935); reprinted from the *Brooklyn Eagle*.

[26] Program of concert "Spirituals to Swing," Carnegie Hall, New York, 23 December 1938, p. 4.

[27] Quoted in Welburn, in Welburn, "American Jazz Criticism," p. 206.

[28] Blesh, *Shining Trumpets*, pp. 163, 289.

[29] Helen Laurenson, "Black and White and Red All Over," *New York* 2/34 (21 August 1978), 36–43.

[30] Chris Albertson, *Bessie* (New York: Stein and Day, 1972), p. 229.

[31] Irving Kolodin, "Number One Swing Man," *Harper's* 179 (September 1939), 431–40.

[32] "Entrepreneur with Crew Cut," *Newsweek* 22/12 (20 September 1943), p. 108–10.

[33] Quoted in Welburn, "American Jazz Criticism," p. 214.

[34] See the relevant entries in John Chilton, *Who's Who of Jazz: Storyville to Swing Street* (London: Chilton Book Company, 1972).

[35] Henry Johnson [John Hammond], "Music," *New Masses* 18/10 (3 March 1986), 27–28.

[36] Ibid., 21/1.

[37] Leonard Feather, *The Jazz Years: Earwitness to an Era* (New York: Da Capo Press, 1987), p. 2.

[38] Chamberlain and Wilson, eds., *The Otis Ferguson Reader*, p. 185.

James Lincoln Collier is a well-known professional writer (if less well-known jazz trombonist) who burst on the jazz-historical scene in 1978 with his book *The Making of Jazz*, which is considered one of the very best one-volume histories of jazz and has been translated into several foreign languages, including Russian and Serbo-Croatian. A National Endowment for the Humanities fellowship partially supported his research toward *Louis Armstrong: An American Genius* (1983), an I.S.A.M. senior research fellowship that toward *Duke Ellington* (1987)—both of them greeted with compliments as well as controversy. The present monograph was developed out of public lectures Collier delivered during his I.S.A.M. fellowship term—"Debunking a Myth: Were Europeans the First to Discover Jazz?" (19 November 1985) and "The Formation of Jazz and the White Americans" (10 December 1985). Its main theses were also sketched in the article "The Faking of Jazz" in the *New Republic* of 18 November 1985.

The Institute for Studies in American Music at Brooklyn College, City University of New York, is a division of the College's Conservatory of Music. It was established in 1971. The Institute contributes to American-music studies in several ways. It publishes a series of monographs, a periodical newsletter, and special publications of various kinds. It serves as an information center and sponsors conferences and symposia dealing with all areas of American music including art music, popular music, and the music of oral tradition. The Institute also encourages and supports research by offering fellowships to distinguished scholars and, for assistance in funded projects, to junior scholars as well. The Institute supervises the series of music editions *Recent Researches in American Music* (published by A–R Editions, Inc.) and is the administrative seat of the Charles Ives Society. I.S.A.M. activities also include presentation of concerts and lectures at Brooklyn College for students, faculty, and the public.